Coding for Children and Young Adults in Libraries

PRACTICAL GUIDES FOR LIBRARIANS

⊚ About the Series

This innovative series written and edited for librarians by librarians provides authoritative, practical information and guidance on a wide spectrum of library processes and operations.

Books in the series are focused, describing practical and innovative solutions to a problem facing today's librarian and delivering step-by-step guidance for planning, creating, implementing, managing, and evaluating a wide range of services and programs.

The books are aimed at beginning and intermediate librarians needing basic instruction/guidance in a specific subject and at experienced librarians who need to gain knowledge in a new area or guidance in implementing a new program/service.

⊚ About the Series Editor

The **Practical Guides for Librarians** series was conceived and edited by M. Sandra Wood, MLS, MBA, AHIP, FMLA, Librarian Emerita, Penn State University Libraries from 2014-2017.

M. Sandra Wood was a librarian at the George T. Harrell Library, the Milton S. Hershey Medical Center, College of Medicine, Pennsylvania State University, Hershey, PA, for over thirty-five years, specializing in reference, educational, and database services. Ms. Wood received an MLS from Indiana University and an MBA from the University of Maryland. She is a fellow of the Medical Library Association and served as a member of MLA's Board of Directors from 1991 to 1995.

Ellyssa Kroski assumed editorial responsibilities for the series beginning in 2017. She is the director of Information Technology at the New York Law Institute as well as an award-winning editor and author of 36 books including *Law Librarianship in the Digital Age* for which she won the AALL's 2014 Joseph L. Andrews Legal Literature Award. Her ten-book technology series, *The Tech Set* won the ALA's Best Book in Library Literature Award in 2011. Ms. Kroski is a librarian, an adjunct faculty member at Drexel and San Jose State University, and an international conference speaker. She has just been named the winner of the 2017 Library Hi Tech Award from the ALA/LITA for her long-term contributions in the area of Library and Information Science technology and its application.

Titles in the Series

1. *How to Teach: A Practical Guide for Librarians* by Beverley E. Crane
2. *Implementing an Inclusive Staffing Model for Today's Reference Services* by Julia K. Nims, Paula Storm, and Robert Stevens

Titles in the Series edited by Ellyssa Kroski

Coding for Children and Young Adults in Libraries

A Practical Guide for Librarians

Wendy Harrop

PRACTICAL GUIDES FOR LIBRARIANS, NO. 45

ROWMAN & LITTLEFIELD
Lanham • Boulder • New York • London

Published by Rowman & Littlefield
An imprint of The Rowman & Littlefield Publishing Group, Inc.
4501 Forbes Boulevard, Suite 200, Lanham, Maryland 20706
www.rowman.com

Unit A, Whitacre Mews, 26-34 Stannary Street, London SE11 4AB

British Library Cataloguing in Publication Information Available

Library of Congress Cataloging-in-Publication Data

Names: Harrop, Wendy, author.
Title: Coding for children and young adults in libraries : a practical guide for librarians / Wendy
Harrop.
Description: Lanham : Rowman & Littlefield, [2018] | Series: Practical guides for librarians ;
no. 45 | Includes bibliographical references and index.
Identifiers: LCCN 2018007361 (print) | LCCN 2018012469 (ebook) | ISBN 9781538108673
| ISBN 9781538108666 (pbk. : alk. paper)
Subjects: LCSH: Computer programming—Study and teaching (Middle school) | Media
programs (Education) | Libraries and teenagers. | Libraries—Activity programs.
Classification: LCC QA76.27 (ebook) | LCC QA76.27 .H37 2018 (print) | DDC
005.1071/2—dc23
LC record available at https://lccn.loc.gov/2018007361

♾️™ The paper used in this publication meets the minimum requirements of American
National Standard for Information Sciences—Permanence of Paper for Printed Library
Materials, ANSI/NISO Z39.48-1992.

Printed in the United States of America

Contents

Preface

It is commonly agreed that computer programming (also known as coding) is an essential fluency for children and young adults in today's society. While schools are implementing this as part of the curriculum, many people will not have had the opportunity for this instruction or need to be taught at a level beyond what a school can offer. Libraries are a key component in teaching computer programming to members of a community.

Coding for Children and Young Adults offers both an experienced opinion about the best ways to set up programs to teach coding and "grab and go" activity ideas for putting coding into action. Readers will learn about many different structures that can be used to set up coding programming in a public library setting, regardless of the size of the library, number of devices available, or experience of the librarians or volunteers. Activities also include literary connections to allow for seamless integration into existing children's, or young adults', library programming. Additionally, *Coding for Children and Young Adults* features activities for integrating coding with makerspace activities, through robotics, LEGOs, and circuitry. As many libraries design makerspaces, maker clubs, and maker events, they will be able to include instruction in computer programming quite naturally.

- Chapter 1 explores the question "What is coding?" We look at the different terms for both coding and coders. We also look briefly at some of the people who influenced the evolution of coding from being something that only career programmers learned to something that children as young as preschool aged are starting to learn.
- Chapter 2 discusses the reasons why every child and young adult should be learning coding at an early age. There are many skills outside of computer programming that can be learned through an understanding of coding concepts. We will also talk about how coding literacy can lead to opportunities in the future for children and young adults, from careers to hobbies.
- Chapter 3 looks specifically at the role that public libraries play in delivering coding programming to the community. The chapter outlines various structures that could be implemented, from one day drop in events to longer multiweek clubs.
- Chapter 4 looks at how to get started. We go through the components needed for a successful program and look at how to make each one happen—from learning how to facilitate a coding program to obtaining materials.

- Chapter 5 goes over the unique considerations when teaching coding to young children. Based on my experience in teaching, I share my thoughts on what to think about when choosing the programs, materials, and structure to best teach young children to code.
- Chapter 6 then moves on to considerations when creating programming for older children and young adults. Because the range of experience with older participants is likely to be broader, there are structures and materials that are likely to work better when teaching these learners.
- Chapter 7 shares many resources for teaching coding without any computers or devices. One of the biggest barriers when setting up a program in a public library is access to enough devices. Building a collection of activities and materials that don't require technology access eliminates that barrier.
- Chapter 8 discusses the applications for coding in makerspaces, as their presence in public libraries continues to grow. Many of the very popular pieces of equipment used in makerspaces, including robots and microprocessors, need coding to be controlled. An understanding of coding expands the options for what one can create in a makerspace environment.
- Lastly, chapter 9 looks at how to reach others through coding programming. Members of underrepresented populations deserve to have the same skills taught to them as everyone else, and public library coding programs are a perfect way to make that happen. Library programs are also a great way to connect with the community, with local schools, and even with others around the globe.

While it is not necessary for librarians to be experts in coding and computer science, it is increasingly necessary for public libraries to be a source of activities, both at the introductory level and beyond, that teach and apply coding knowledge. There are many coding courses available for individuals to take on their own; however, the integration of the coding knowledge to projects, events, and community activities is what makes the learning meaningful. This book will help libraries move confidently into offering programming that is appropriate and engaging for participants of many different ages and experience levels.

Acknowledgments

During the time between when I started writing this book and when I finished it, I was constantly learning about new materials, apps, devices, and toys that had entered the market. Such is the nature with a technology topic, I suppose. In an attempt to share as broad a spectrum of ideas as possible, I went to the experts—the teachers and librarians who are running very creative and successful programs in their communities. In talking with them about what they have found works best, I learned so many new things that I will now implement into my programs. Thank you to those who were willing to share their expertise with me along the way.

Much gratitude to Ellyssa, the reason I was ever published in the first place. By crowdsourcing teachers and librarians for her 2017 book *The Makerspace Librarian's Sourcebook*, she gave me an opportunity to share some of what I've loved doing with my students in our makerspace over the past four years. To follow that with this opportunity, to help schools and libraries provide programming so that everyone can learn to code, has been an experience of great growth and learning.

Most importantly, so much love and gratitude to my husband, Joe, and my sons, Sam and Zach, who put up with a year of me being in front of my computer working to bring this book to fruition. Thank you for your support, your patience, and your encouragement.

What Is Coding?

"Technology is not a separate discipline that can be considered in isolation from other aspects of society; it's interwoven with every aspect of our existence. Learning to code is a pathway to full participation in the modern workforce and in public life."
—TONY SMITH, FORMER SUPERINTENDENT, OAKLAND UNIFIED SCHOOL DISTRICT (CODE.ORG N.D.)

Anyone who works in or near technology education, libraries, or schools has likely heard something about coding in the last five years. In 2013 with the introduction of the Hour of Code initiative that aimed to get every student in schools participating in some kind of coding activity for at least an hour, teachers and librarians began to take notice. The term *coding* is starting to be heard outside of school and library settings now as well. This is not just a trend in the United States. Schools all over the world are implementing computer science education into their programming. Schools in England are actually including coding in the public school curriculum for all students starting at age five (Cuthbertson 2014).

SCHOOLS ARE RAPIDLY INTEGRATING coding into their curricula, and public libraries and makerspaces are offering face-to-face coding classes, clubs, and events to expose their patrons to various coding programs. Technology companies are racing, from the other side, to create apps, games, sites, and toys that help teach coding to users of all ages. This has resulted in a wide variety of tools available to teach learners of all ages. It has also led to a plethora of low-tech coding toys and games, thus bringing the price point for obtaining materials down and providing learning options regardless of what devices are available.

⟳ Defining "Coding"

Coding is also referred to as programming, computer science, or development. Those who write code are referred to as coders, programmers, developers, or computer scientists. When we speak about the skill in terms of younger children or beginners, we typically refer to it as coding. At the most basic level, coding is writing a sequence of commands in a programming language to input into a computer. These commands can control things like appearance, function, and movement. This practice became referred to as coding, because the sequence of commands is known as the *source code* for the program. And putting the commands together is known as *writing code*, which has been shortened to coding. And while decades ago, the only people who knew how to write code were the programmers and developers behind the computer hardware and software that were just becoming part of the mainstream, now there's a belief that all children, young adults, and even adults beyond school ages can benefit from understanding the fundamentals of coding.

Figure 1.1. Students engage in digital coding activities.

When writing code, programmers put symbols, words, and phrases together in certain sequences. The words and phrases that make up the code depend on which programming language is being used, as each language has its own unique meanings for symbols and sequences. A series of symbols in a particular sequence creates an algorithm. The algorithms comprise a program, which is designed to perform a specific function, like develop the content for an app or a web page.

Although computer programming has been a part of technology development for quite a long time, the earlier forms of programming involved writing the program externally (on paper or cards) and then inputting it into the computer. As computers evolved, so did programming, until programs could be typed directly into the computer for processing. This made it more efficient and accessible. With computers becoming a part of every classroom, every library, and every household, there became a desire for the layperson to learn how to write and understand code—for the purpose of developing web pages and software, but also for troubleshooting and debugging previously written code. Understanding how to write, interpret, and troubleshoot code has become increasingly important in many careers. Most businesses use a web page for advertising, soliciting patrons, or sales of products. These sites need to be appealing, user friendly, and reliable. None of those things can happen without well-written code. Of course those without a computer science background could hire a programmer or a web designer to do these tasks for them, but wouldn't it be more efficient to be able to handle that themselves?

WHAT CAN YOU DO WITH CODING?

- Make your own website
- Become a career programmer
- Start a business
- Understand how computers work

(Code Conquest n.d.)

Part of the appeal of coding in academic settings is that it is the perfect combination of logical reasoning and creating. The concept of writing a sequence of commands to manipulate something appeals to those who are technology minded, but the way it allows creators to work in a digital medium appeals as well to those who are more creative minded. It is a way for a programmer—whether amateur or experienced—to bring an idea or a design to fruition, much like an author creates written work from a series of notes and ideas, or an artist creates a piece to represent a vision. For example, a young child may want to animate a digital character within a program to represent a favorite character from a book. Manipulating source code can allow this child to bring the picture in his or her brain to life on the screen. Or a young entrepreneur designing a web page to market a business can be sure that the appearance of the site gives the right impression for the business. The practical applications for coding are endless, and with the development of new sites, programs, courses, and games, it has become increasingly easier for anyone to learn.

⊚ The History of Computer Programming

If we went into great detail about the history of programming, it would constitute an entire book of its own. The evolution from pre-computer era programming through military programming into a science that nonmilitary organizations began employing encompasses many decades, many brilliant minds, and many new technologies along the way. Of course, all of that was before noncareer programmers began to learn to write code, and programming became more of a mainstream activity. There are a few individuals important to mention, though, for their particular impact on coding as it pertains to young people, schools, and libraries.

Ada Lovelace

While coding is not new, many of us did not know much about it until recently, when it became so common. There are decades of computer science and programming history before its recent popularity—even programming as a means of controlling a device long before computers and tablets were even around. As a matter of fact, the first published program was written by a woman by the name of Ada Lovelace. She began programming in the mid-1800s. She was creating programs using punched cards that told a machine what to do. This established a practice for how to program devices. The first widely used applications of programming weren't seen until World War II, when computers were used to break code-encrypted messages from enemy troops. Much has changed in the world of computer programming since then.

Seymour Papert

You can't talk about the history of computer programming or coding without discussion about Massachusetts Institute of Technology (MIT) and the great Seymour Papert. Papert is most well known for his theory of constructionism in education. The constructionist theory is that as information goes into a child's head, if he or she doesn't interact with the new information in some sort of a sensory manner, the child won't learn from it. Papert put great weight on the importance of creation—whether that be building, drawing, or even coding—as a means to understand what is being learned. This led him to create a visual programming language called Logo that asked users to give directions to a "turtle" on the screen to control what the turtle did. The goal was to create a programming language that could be used with children to help develop their problem-solving and creativity skills. Papert also started the department at MIT that later became the MIT Media Lab, home of the Lifelong Kindergarten group. Later, he also worked with LEGO to develop the LEGO Mindstorms Robotics kit. His work, as well as works influenced by him, have been, and continue to be, used around the world.

Mitch Resnick

Well known among those in the coding world is another gentleman from MIT named Mitch Resnick. He has always been at the front of the movement to develop computer science education in his work with his team in Boston. He believes that one of the most important life skills we need to develop in our children is the ability to think creatively. And he feels that there is no better example of this than watching students in kindergarten. He observed kindergarteners playing and creating, imagining and learning—not through texts, not through direct instruction from the teacher, but through play. He felt that unstructured creative play was the way to truly develop thinkers, and that such play was no longer a big part of the school day. This led to the creation of his Lifelong Kindergarten research group at MIT in Boston. This group works out of a media lab that is filled with technology, gadgets, nontraditional learning spaces, and researchers busy playing, experimenting, trying, and creating. Many familiar creations have come out of the Lifelong Kindergarten group, such as LEGO Robotics and Scratch.

"The ability to code computer programs is an important part of literacy in today's society. When people learn to code in Scratch, they learn important strategies for solving problems, designing projects, and communicating ideas."—Mitch Resnick (Scratch n.d.)

During the time when smartphones, tablets, and inexpensive PCs made their way into the hands of a generation of young people, a term was being used to describe this generation—Digital Natives. The reasoning behind this term was that this generation had been born into a very technologically advanced society, and they would be fluent in its use from a very young age. As Resnick began to observe young people and their use of technology, however, he noted that they were, in fact, extremely comfortable using technology for interactions—with the Internet, with friends, with various programs—but they were not fluent in creating on their computers. He felt that until that changed, something would be missing. This led to the focus on developing a way for users to create, and thus was born the programming environment of Scratch, a direct descendent of the Logo programming language of decades before.

How Coding Works

At the beginning of a program, a starting action is established (e.g., "When run"). The starting action, often called a *run command*, will vary based on the coding language and the purpose of the program. Then the program will tell the computer what input or data to look for, and from what source it will be coming. Within the lines of code, the programmer will have indicated what decision will be made based on the input, similar to an "If . . . then . . ." structure. This will result in some sort of output given back from the computer. Then the program will indicate how many times the sequence (or loop) should be repeated and what exceptions might be encountered.

Programming Languages

"My first coding class was in Basic, designing a circulation program for my library. Times have changed since then!"—Kim Bannigan, technology coordinator, DeForest School District, Wisconsin

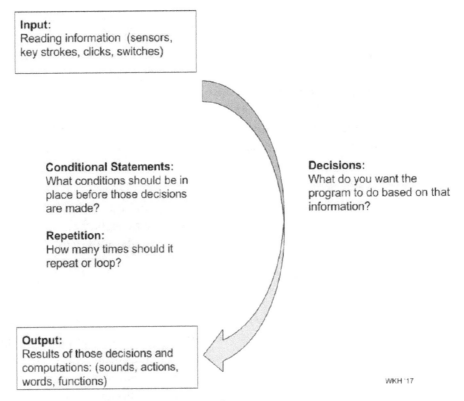

Input:
Reading information (sensors, key strokes, clicks, switches)

Conditional Statements:
What conditions should be in place before those decisions are made?

Repetition:
How many times should it repeat or loop?

Decisions:
What do you want the program to do based on that information?

Output:
Results of those decisions and computations: (sounds, actions, words, functions)

WKH '17

Figure 1.2. Coding follows a certain flow.

There are many different coding languages, each designed to perform a specific function. Those of us who are not in the programming field will likely never know, or even hear of, most of the thousands of languages in existence. We are likely, though, to know many of the same ones as other people in the fields of library sciences and education. While it is not essential to know most or all of the coding languages, it is important to have a basic level of familiarity with some of the more commonly known programming languages that are out there. Some of these languages are what we know of as *visual programming languages* (sometimes called either VPLs or block coding languages), which use blocks similar to puzzle pieces to connect and form programs. Others are known as are *text-based programming languages.* They rely on specific words and symbols, combined in a specific sequence to provide the computer with instructions. The languages we tend to use more with young people, like Scratch, Python, JavaScript, and Blockly, are easier languages for someone just starting out learning programming. Once users are comfortable, some might graduate to the more challenging languages like Perl and C++.

Coding languages can be described as well in terms of their ease of use. We refer to them as low level or high level. Low-level languages are named as such because they are the most similar to binary language, which seems simpler but is actually harder for most humans to understand. High-level languages have more symbols, terms, and conventions, but this makes these languages easier to learn, particularly for young people.

Visual Programming Languages

Visual programming languages, or block programming languages, are favorites of those working with young learners, primarily because they are easier to learn, since they don't

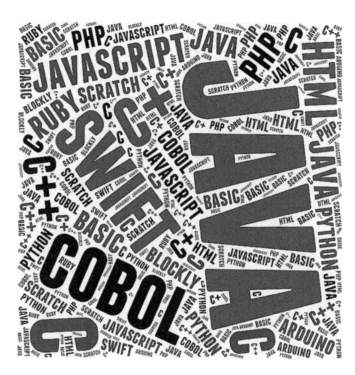

Figure 1.3. There are many different coding languages, each of which has a distinct purpose. *Courtesy of Wikimedia Commons*

rely on text and they are visually engaging. These languages translate lines of text-based code into visual blocks that can be dragged across the screen and "hooked" together to create sequences of commands. The blocks of commands control a particular character or background element on the screen.

Scratch

Scratch was introduced to the programming world in 2003. It was one of the first block programming platforms. The original versions were much simpler looking than the current version, lacking color and somewhat limited in the variety of blocks available. Scratch was released in a broader scale in 2007, and it immediately became a favorite of many in the position of teaching young people how to code.

Kodu

Kodu is a visual programming language that was created by Microsoft. It is designed to work on either a PC or an Xbox, and it works well for creating 3D games. It is very popular among amateur game designers.

Blockly

Blockly is another visual coding language that uses drag-and-drop blocks to create animations or program external devices, such as robots or drones. Blockly was developed by Google for use programming objects like robots, drones, and microprocessors in makerspaces.

Text-Based Programming Languages

JavaScript

If you are learning coding for the purpose of website design, you'll likely become familiar with JavaScript. As a matter of fact, JavaScript is the most widely known coding language in the world (Code Conquest n.d.). Code written in JavaScript is able to be read and translated in many web browsers, like Google Chrome, Safari, or Firefox. This makes it a good language for those looking to customize the appearance, layout, or functions of web pages.

Ruby

Ruby is a relatively young programming language, being developed within the last thirty years. It was designed with the intent that it was a teaching language for those wanting to learn how to program. It is used for designing dynamic web pages as well as controlling external objects, like microprocessors or robots.

Python

Python is thought to be one of the easier text-based coding languages. For that reason, many people just starting out in programming begin by learning Python. It is a fairly easy code to read—the symbols and syntax used can be understood quite easily if the user is somewhat familiar with the basic conventions of coding. Python is the language used most often to program Raspberry Pi microcomputers.

Swift

Swift has more recently entered the programming scene, having been developed by Apple in the early 2010s for the purpose of making programming for Apple devices more streamlined. It immediately became one of the most popular and well-loved programming languages among users.

Perl

Perl is designed to help the computer process text. It was originally meant to be used primarily for programming in the Unix operating system, but has since been used more widely for graphics and animation programming, among other things.

C

One of the most difficult coding languages to learn, C is what powers most computer operating systems that we use today. It is also one of the most widely used coding languages, as it powers many of the programs and systems we are very familiar with.

C++

Many video games are written in C++. It is a more evolved version of C and allows for use on a variety of hardware platforms. It is used primarily for app and game development and continues to be a commonly learned language.

Visual Basic

Visual Basic was designed by Microsoft in the 1990s with the purpose of programming reactions to specific actions like mouse clicks or hitting certain keys. It is a widely learned programming language among those writing programs for use within Windows. It is very popular among those programmers without a computer science background.

PROS AND CONS OF TEXT-BASED PROGRAMMING LANGUAGES

Pros:

- Useful for writing web pages, designing games, and creating apps
- Many can run on a large variety of operating systems
- Standard structures for writing code make interpreting code in languages like Python and JavaScript fairly easy

Cons:

- Each employs a different set of symbols and purposes
- Syntax errors render the program ineffective
- Complexity makes them too complicated for use with most young children

---

As libraries and schools incorporate coding clubs, app development classes, maker-spaces, and robotics into their programming, it is important that facilitators have a good understanding of languages being used to code various equipment, in order to be able to assist patrons who are having trouble, and to instruct new users to help them get started. It is not important for facilitators to know every coding language, but understanding the basic conventions of source code and the most commonly used languages will be very helpful. This is becoming easier to do as online courses are showing up everywhere, are usually free, and are often self-paced, making coding accessible to adult learners as well.

Key Points

- *Coding*, *computer programming*, and *computer science* are terms that are often used interchangeably, although they refer to very different things.
- In the last few decades, computer programming has become popular among developers outside of the computer science fields.
- Coding is the process of putting words and symbols into a particular sequence in order to tell a computer what function to perform.
- The first computer programmer was Ada Lovelace, who programmed in the 1840s.
- Commonly used coding languages can be labeled as *visual programming languages* or *text-based programming languages*.

Resources

Blockly—https://developers.google.com/blockly/. Google site for learning and sharing projects using Blockly

Kodu—https://www.kodugamelab.com/

Perl—https://www.perl.org/

Python—https://www.python.org/

Ruby—https://www.ruby-lang.org/en/

Scratch—https://scratch.mit.edu/

ScratchEd—http://scratched.gse.harvard.edu/. Online community for sharing ideas, resources, and activities

Swift—https://developer.apple.com/swift/

References

Code.org. N.d. "Leaders and Trend-Setters All Agree on One Thing." https://code.org/quotes.

CodeConquest. N.d. "Benefits of Learning Coding." Retrieved from http://www.codeconquest.com/what-is-coding/benefits/.

Wikipedia. 2017. S.v. "Coding Conventions." *Wikipedia, the Free Encyclopedia*. Retrieved from https://en.wikipedia.org/wiki/Coding_conventions.

Why Teach Coding?

"Coding may not be for every child, but the choice is for every student. When you teach coding to early learners, you create an incubator. Students deserve the option to get involved in computer science."

—HADI PARTOVI (DAVIS 2013)

Why Is Coding Important?

IN THE EDUCATION WORLD, there is an ongoing argument about whether coding (computer science) should be required curriculum. Most educators and administrators agree that computer literacy is important for all students to learn, but the issue is when and how it will be taught during an already full academic year. Schools are moving away from teaching technology as a stand-alone curriculum, and computer labs are being dismantled to allow for more devices to be moved into classrooms so that technology can be integrated across the subjects. So without designated technology instruction, there isn't an open block of time to teach coding. This is where public libraries become a hugely important piece of the puzzle. More and more public libraries are filling this gap. They are not bound to academic standards, time constraints, building-wide schedules, or educational legislation. They have the freedom to use any devices available to them to offer computer science education to the public through coding clubs, classes, and seminars. Kids, young adults, even adults can participate in coding activities, programs and clubs outside of a traditional school or work day, and in a comfortable, supportive environment.

But why is coding important? Why do teachers and administrators feel it is vital? Coding is behind so much of what we do throughout our days, whether on a computer, a smartphone, or even a remote control. Coding is not just learning the language used to program. So many skills are addressed and developed as a user learns to program. Mitch Resnick, creator of Scratch, said that in the creation of the program, their goal was to help children become fluent in a new technology—help them feel comfortable expressing themselves with the new technology. He feels that this is critical in today's computer science education in order to open up other opportunities for learning (TED 2013).

"A background in computer science provides a strong foundation for nearly any career path in any industry in the 21st century economy."—Todd Young, US Senator, Indiana (Code.org n.d.)

Usually if you ask computer science teachers why we need to make sure young people are learning how to code, the first response relates to career readiness. Right now there are career opportunities available in the world of technology and computer science that did not exist a decade ago. The Internet continues to grow in its importance to everyday life. To the consumer, those apps and web pages that make life easier by allowing us to do our shopping, banking, communicating and even education online are all well designed and user friendly. When we design our own web pages using something like Google Sites, Wix, or Weebly, it is so easy—we drag and drop various features onto our page; we upload and import media from a number of sources. What we take for granted is that every single color, word, design, action, button, or link on that page is doing what we want it to do, or looking how we want it to look, because someone has written extensive code to make that happen. Have you ever looked at the HTML source on a web page? The many lines of code, which look to most of us like gibberish, are telling the computer exactly what to do and when. Although this is much more advanced than our children and young adults are ready for, it all starts with the basics—the fundamental understanding of how to program, and that is what we need to be teaching through our library and school programs.

In addition to the many careers we have available in science, technology, engineering, and math (STEM) fields right now, our young people will have options that we have not even thought of yet. And although the number of available STEM and computer science jobs is projected to continue growing steadily, the number of people entering the STEM and computer science work field continues to decrease (Code.org n.d.). We need to ensure that we are creating and training the workers, engineers, thinkers, and programmers who will be ready for wherever technology goes next. It is very shortsighted of us to think only of giving our young people the skills that they need for the jobs we know of today. Twenty years ago, we didn't have tablets, and thirty years ago we didn't have smartphones. Now there are millions of them—often as many as two to three per person in a household. With the growth in use of these mobile devices has come the need for app developers. There is a need for proficient programmers who can take a person's, or a company's, vision and turn it into a useful, functional, user-friendly application. The automation of many of the household items we use daily requires programming—the

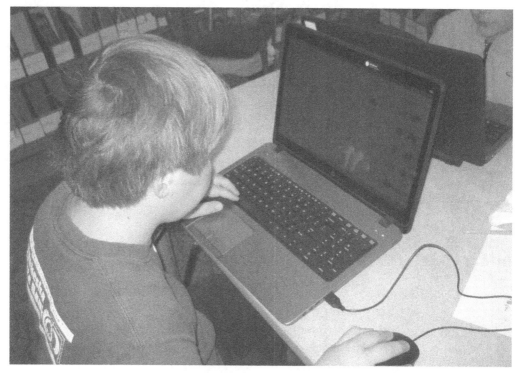

Figure 2.1. It is important to teach youth to code at an early age.

refrigerator that talks to us; smart televisions that can access the Internet through our wireless network; smart controls in our vehicles that talk to our telephones, keep us safe, alert us to hazards—these have all been programmed. And that programming starts with an understanding of basic coding. If we are not providing the opportunity to learn the basics of programming, we are doing ourselves, and our future STEM and technology experts, a great disservice.

The reality is, technology is not going away. It will inevitably grow and evolve as today's children and young adults enter the workforce. An understanding of how to use various devices, programs, and apps is not going to be enough. To understand how they work, and why, will allow for a greater understanding of how to develop future technologies. Understanding how to debug and troubleshoot will enable us to continue to grow in our use of technology to improve our lives.

CAREER PATHS REQUIRING CODING EXPERIENCE

- Website design
- App development
- Video game development
- Computer animation
- Engineering
- Information technology
- Network management
- Software design
- Database management
- Software testing and quality assurance

What Technological Skills Are Taught through Coding?

Programming

Participating in coding activities from a young age provides users the opportunity to develop a firm understanding of the components of basic coding—input, output, arithmetic, conditionals, and loops (see chapter 1). Although visual coding programs, which employ the use of color coded blocks that the user drags onto a workspace to build code, are much simpler than writing code in a language such as Python or JavaScript, users are still using these components to create the code. Students can practice the structure of effective and efficient code early and often, so that once they are ready, they do not have to start from scratch to learn another coding language.

Integration of Technology and Engineering

Learning to write, read, and debug code moves a user from being a consumer of the technology to being a producer and developer of the technology. Programming is designed to control or automate something. This understanding can be carried over into the study of engineering. Users can create designs that will ultimately be controlled through code that they've written.

App and Game Design

One of the most popular applications of programming right now is in the development of games and apps for download onto various devices or for playing online. Programs like Scratch, Tynker, and Sploder encourage users to create games and make them public, so that they can be used by other players (see chapter 6). Through Android and iOS app stores, developers can market programs that they have created—game apps, as well as apps to simplify everyday tasks, fitness apps, and more.

Website Design

Behind every web page we visit is code. Someone (or a team of people) wrote that code. Skilled programmers and developers with a secure understanding of how to write code as well as how to debug code when errors occur are constantly in need to create an attractive and engaging Internet presence for companies, individuals, and small businesses. While there are many sites on which individuals can create their own web pages, they are somewhat limited. To have a truly dynamic site, a proficient programmer is needed.

What Nontechnological Skills Are Taught through Coding?

Most people will agree that those wanting to go into a STEM career will need a strong background in computer science and a secure knowledge of programming languages. It can be argued, however, that the skills acquired through learning coding are not only beneficial to STEM careers, but to all careers. There are specific skills taught in computer science instruction that can be applied across many different areas. All coding, no matter what language, no matter what program, app, game, or activity, involves computational

Figure 2.2. Why we need to teach coding.

thinking—a way of looking at something that applies three very important skills: cause and effect, sequence, and troubleshooting (reviewing for errors). It is safe to say that these skills are not limited to STEM and technology careers.

Cause and Effect

The basis of programming is the use of conditional statements—those that establish a cause-and-effect relationship: if I do _____, then the computer should do _____. (For example, if I enter a certain numerical code, then I will get a certain result on the page.) Understanding cause-and-effect relationships and being able to alter one to influence the other is essential for any sort of problem solving, relationship building, or design. As a teacher and a parent, I strive to get my students and my children to understand this: "Your action led to this result." "What you said caused this to happen." "If you try doing this differently, you may see a different result." Seeing situations from this viewpoint takes practice, whether the situation in question is social or academic. If children at a young age learn how to identify and review the cause-and-effect through coding, they will undoubtedly develop resilience as a result. Rather than giving up when something doesn't work, or doesn't go their way, they can look at the cause and figure out what to do differently to effect change. This also develops strong analytical skills as they look at different possible options to determine which will cause the result they desire. When the coding activity is being done in pairs or teams, it also helps kids develop important communication and negotiation skills. I would very comfortably argue that there are few jobs and few roles in society where this isn't helpful.

Sequence

Lines of code written in the wrong order will not yield the desired result. Writing properly sequenced code requires very organized and logical thinking and planning. Again, this is a habit that, once learned, will carry over into many academic areas—writing, science, math, music, and more. Outside of school, this will also help with engineering, building, and construction projects. This act of sequencing ideas is also helpful in building language skills.

Debugging

One of the most important skills of a successful programmer is the ability to problem-solve and debug a program to find out why it is not working. It requires very careful and thorough review of lines of code and syntax, as well as a detailed understanding of the language itself. This kind of *reverse thinking*—identifying the problem from an existing program and fixing it—is an excellent example of higher-level thinking, perfect to challenge and engage those young people who find their school learning tedious and boring. Debugging in pairs or in teams also reinforces some great communication skills, like negotiation, listening, and collaborating.

Problem Solving

Writing code from scratch, on the other hand, applies a different kind of problem solving: programmers are thinking about the end result—what do they want the program to do—and coming up with the proper commands and sequence to yield the desired result. Taking that a step further, if the programmer is fluent in more than one programming language, he or she will need to evaluate which language suits the purpose of the problem at hand.

Mathematical Skills

In the United States, the focus in mathematics instruction has shifted from learning how to *do* specific types of mathematical tasks to learning how to *think mathematically* and approach problems. One of the Common Core State Standards for Mathematics Practice is that students should make sense of problems and persevere in solving them. As discussed previously, much of programming is identifying the problem and deciding how to solve it—what instructions will be needed to produce the intended result. Along with that, the testing and debugging of programs practices that skill of perseverance in mathematical problem solving. So regardless of where a child is learning how to code, the positive effects will be seen in his or her mathematics work in school.

> CCSS.MATH.PRACTICE.MP1 Make sense of problems and persevere in solving them.
>
> —United States Common Core State Standard for Mathematical Practice (Common Core State Standards Initiative n.d.)

Parallels to Literature and Storytelling

Libraries have long offered programming around literature—from story-time activities for young children to book clubs for adults and young adults. What better place to explore the connections between coding and literature. Both require a certain structure, and deviation from that structure makes it difficult or impossible for the user (reader) to make sense of what is being communicated. Both also require a starting point and an end point. Attention to detail and precise word choice ensure that the desired response is achieved. When young children are taught to write stories, they are taught to identify the problem and then write the steps that make up the solution. This is no different than writing a program to solve a problem with technology. Some of the coding activities that might be used with younger children might involve creating an animation—why not have them animate a story or a character from literature?

The skills that can be learned and reinforced through learning coding go beyond just learning how to make the turtle move or how to print "Hello World." There are connections throughout their home and school lives, as well as skills they will need for their futures. To ignore the need for them to learn coding starting at a young age would be doing them a great disservice. "Will every job involve programming? No. But it is crucial we equip future generations to think about the world in a new way" (Crow 2014).

Key Points

Coding prepares children and young adults for many future careers.

Coding teaches technological skills like app development, web design, and network management.

Coding also teaches essential work and thinking skills like problem solving, persistence, sequence, and cause-and-effect relationships.

Coding offers connections to school curriculum, so learning to program can improve performance in traditional school subjects.

References

Code.org. N.d. "Leaders and Trend-Setters All Agree on One Thing." Retrieved from https://code.org/quotes.

Common Core State Standards Initiative. N.d. "Standards for Mathematical Practice." CoreStandards.org. Retrieved from http://www.corestandards.org/Math/Practice/.

Crow, Dan. 2014. "Why Every Child Should Learn to Code." *Guardian*, February 7. Retrieved from http://www.theguardian.com/technology/2014/feb/07/year-of-code-dan-crow-songkick.

Davis, Vicki. 2013. "15+ Ways of Teaching Every Student to Code (Even without—Edutopia)." Edutopia, December 4. Retrieved from https://www.edutopia.org/blog/15-ways-teaching-students-coding-vicki-davis.

TED. 2013. "Mitch Resnick: Let's Teach Kids to Code." YouTube video, January 29. https://www.youtube.com/watch?v=Ok6LbV6bqaE.

CHAPTER 3

The Role of Libraries in Learning to Code

IN THIS CHAPTER

▷ Why Are Libraries Implementing Coding Programs?

▷ What Do Library Programs Look Like?

"Libraries are arguably the single most important grass-roots community space with capacity to provide ALL members of their community access to current knowledge and information. They can provide Internet-enabled computers and tablets, collaborative working spaces, themed activities and programs targeting different audiences and acquire new resources to add to their borrowing collections."
—ADAM SELINGER, CHILDREN'S DISCOVERY MUSEUM, SYDNEY, AUSTRALIA
(AUSTRALIAN PUBLIC LIBRARY ALLIANCE 2017)

Why Are Libraries Implementing Coding Programs?

IN THE PAST, libraries were primarily a source of reading material and informational material, with some community programming usually centered on literature or current events. With so much reading material and information now being available online, the role of libraries in the community has shifted. They are still a place for information, but often, now, that information is in the form of courses, clubs, workshops, or access to technology. This is true when we look at providing coding instruction to the community. In an attempt to provide an opportunity to learn programming to all members of a community, libraries have become a key part of the equation. Some libraries are opting to offer coding classes, some sponsor coding clubs, some are setting up mentor relationships between programmers and community members, and some are hosting one-day codeathon events. No matter what is being offered, the outcome is bound to be valuable for participants.

Schools Are Unable to Meet the Need

As the emphasis on standardized testing and increasingly complex curriculum take up more of school teachers' time during the school year, curricula like computer science and coding are being pushed to the bottom of the list. We know that programming is a skill that young people should be learning, and we see that the earlier in their lives they can start learning to code, the more fluent they will become at programming, but it is becoming more and more difficult to meet this need. For this reason, a partnership with local libraries is becoming an essential component to this learning. Even if a library can't offer a multiyear, intensive coding curriculum, early exposure to coding through a club or a class can build the foundation for further learning later.

High-Interest Programming

Many times, understanding of programming leads to the opportunity for some very high-interest activities. Libraries are offering app development classes and clubs, where participants are learning how to code with the end goal of creating an app. In some cases, this app might be produced for personal use, but for others, creating an app and then marketing it through online stores like the iTunes App Store or the Google Play App Store might be the foot in the door that a budding entrepreneur needs to start a future career.

Take, for example, Ethan Duggan, of Las Vegas, Nevada. At age eleven, Ethan had taken some coding courses and learned how to design apps for his smartphone. One of his ideas took hold and became an immediate hit—the Lazy Dad app. He followed it with creation of five more apps and has since spoken at large venues like the South by Southwest (SXSW) conference and secured his future as a designer. Now, four years later, Ethan is employed as a software developer despite being only a teen. There are many such stories out there, about both adults and young people launching careers and making sizable fortunes because of their coding fluency (Koetsier 2013).

Access for All in the Community

These should be opportunities available to everyone, regardless of where they live, what school they go to, whether they have computer access at home, or whether they are beyond school age. Public libraries are a place of equal access for members of the community, and they are increasingly a source of extended learning programs, after-school clubs, and community outreach programs. This makes them the ideal hub for learning a valuable skill like computer programming in a way that is accommodating to schedules, financial situations, and school experiences.

College- and Career-Readiness Skills

The role of a community should be to take care of its own. As such, we want to be sure we are providing our young people with the best opportunities in their futures. We want to provide them with activities that help them nurture and develop the work and social skills that they will need regardless of what they choose to do in their adult lives. We

Figure 3.1. Coding programs in libraries reach many adult and youth members of a community.

want to be sure we are opening up opportunities for them, whether that is by providing the skill set they will need or exposing them to careers they didn't even know were possible. Coding clubs in libraries are an opportunity for every member of the community to have an introduction to coding, and possibly even an opportunity to talk with a mentor in a programming-related field. Libraries offering coding curriculum are also a great resource for educators who want or need to learn how to code in order to then include that instruction in their classroom curriculum. Rather than a teacher needing to take a university course in programming for a large tuition cost, a low-cost program through the local library opens up the possibility of getting more of the teachers in a community fluent in programming as well.

Teaching Coding through Games

Have you ever heard of Minecraft? Sploder? Roblox? These immensely popular gaming sites are some of the many places that our young people are already applying coding. They are creating worlds, designing and sharing games, and modifying projects that others have shared. This is a real-life instance of coding in their day-to-day activity. We should be taking advantage of that and using the opportunity to increase the depth of their coding by hosting challenges, competitions, showcases, or festivals where coders are invited to share what they make with others. Having a real audience for their creations increases the level of effort and complexity that they are likely to put into a project. It's also an opportunity to get to know about their prior knowledge and comfort level, and what types

Figure 3.2. The characteristics of a Future Ready Librarian. *Courtesy of Wikimedia Commons*

of activities should be planned so that participants are pushed to the next level in their coding experience.

Schools are often using Minecraft in their technology classes, but not usually many other programs. Other coding-related games are usually learned by children and young people with computer and Internet access at home. Libraries offer the same opportunity to those without computers at home. The partnership between schools and libraries in delivering instruction is detailed further in the Future Ready Schools and Future Ready Librarians programs (see the resources section).

"Future Ready Librarians will provide resources, strategies, and connections for district leaders and librarians to be able to work together to promote and implement innovative learning opportunities for students" (Dossin n.d.).

◎ What Do Library Coding Programs Look Like?

There is no one right format for designing a coding course. Libraries need to look at their device availability and their clientele to determine what will work best. Following are some examples of how various libraries are providing coding programming to their patrons.

Variety Is Key: The Toronto Public Library

The mission of the Toronto Public Library, as stated in their current Four Year Strategic Plan, is to increase access and opportunity for their patrons. They work toward meeting this need by offering a wide variety of courses, both multiweek and "pop-up" one-week sessions. Their pop-up sessions are overviews of one particular coding language, or specific to a piece of equipment. Kids' courses integrate some sort of STEM or maker challenge, like LEGO challenges, for example (Toronto Public Library n.d.).

Project_<Code>: New York Public Library

Young adults in the New York City area can take part in a ten-week coding class focusing on web page design languages—HTML, CSS, and more. Participants can leave the class with a good foundational understanding of code and how to use it to design web pages, opening up career possibilities for many of them, and introducing a hobby for others (New York Public Library n.d.).

Coding Meet-Ups: The Phoenix Public Library

The Burton Barr Central Branch of the Phoenix Public Library has turned its entire fourth floor into a makerspace. Within this space they host many different activities, many involving coding. One that offers great opportunities for young adults is their JavaScript meetup. Participants are invited to share ideas, ask questions, and meet mentors focusing on coding with JavaScript (Phoenix Public Library n.d.).

Coding Competitions: The Saratoga Public Library

Saratoga Public Library, in Saratoga, California, recently hosted a Teen Hackathon. Teens were encouraged to sign up in teams of three to five to participate in the one-day event. The objective was to develop original code to address a current social issue, like bullying for example. Teams spent the day coding before presenting their project to a panel of judges. Winning teams received cash prizes (Santa Clara County Library District 2017).

No Tech Needed: Harold Washington Library Center, Chicago Public Library

In the children's section of the Harold Washington Library in Chicago, there is a play room filled with nondigital toys that teach coding concepts and computational thinking. These toys include Beebots, LEGO WeDo sets, Cubetto Robots, and several toys that are the product of Learning Beautiful, a startup company connected with the Media Lab at MIT. The philosophy behind this space is that this is the age at which kids are developing print literacy and language structure, so they can also be developing computational literacy (problem solving, sequencing, breaking problems into smaller parts) at the same time. As the availability of nondigital toys increases, the collection for a room like this could continually be growing (Jackson 2017).

Agenda:

8:30-9:00: Idea brain-storming

9:00-12:00: Coding time

12-12:30 Lunch break

12:30-3:15: Continue coding

3:15-3:30: Prepare for 5-7 min presentation with Q&A

3:30-3:45: Break

3:45-4:30: Team presentations

4:30-4:40: Panelist review of presentations

4:40-5:00: Award Presentation

Areas:
- The hack (s) should solve problems in one of the following areas:
  - Anti-bullying
  - Improving environment
  - Help people filter fake news articles or posts
  - Ideas to foster diversity on campus/at workplace

Figure 3.3. Saratoga, California, Library hackathon agenda. *Courtesy of Santa Clara County Libraries, www.sccl.org*

🌀 Key Points

- Coding is a high-interest subject, and patrons can participate in fun activities and camps when provided by the libraries.
- Future-ready schools and librarians need to work in partnership to be able to deliver curriculum to young people.
- Providing opportunities to learn programming in libraries allows for all members of the community to have the same access to instruction.
- Libraries have many options for what coding offerings could involve.

🌀 Resources

Future Ready Librarians—http://futureready.org/program-overview/librarians/
Minecraft Education Edition—https://education.minecraft.net/
Sploder—http://www.sploder.com/
Roblox—https://www.roblox.com/
Learning Beautiful—http://learningbeautiful.com

References

Australian Public Library Alliance. 2017. *How Public Libraries Contribute to the STEM Agenda 2017*. Canberra, Australia: Australian Library and Information Association. Retrieved from https://read.alia.org.au/sites/default/files/documents/how_public_libraries_contribute_to_the_stem_agenda_2017.pdf.

Dossin, Lia. N.d. "Future Ready Librarians." Future Ready Schools. Retrieved from http://future-ready.org/program-overview/librarians/.

Jackson, Cheryl V. 2017. "Toys at Chicago Public Library Teach Building Blocks of Code—without a Computer." *Chicago Tribune*, August 3. Retrieved from http://www.chicagotribune.com/bluesky/originals/ct-bsi-library-coding-toys-20170803-story.html.

Koetsier, John. 2013. "This 12-Year-Old Kid Learned to Code on Codecademy, Built 5 Apps, and Is Speaking at SXSW." Venture Beat. Retrieved from https://venturebeat.com/2013/08/14/this-12-year-old-kid-learned-to-code-on-codecademy-built-5-apps-and-is-speaking-at-sxsw/.

New York Public Library. N.d. "TechConnect: About Us." Retrieved from https://sites.google.com/a/nypl.org/techconnect/about-us.

Phoenix Public Library. N.d. "Teens: MACH1 Programs." Retrieved from https://www.phoenix-publiclibrary.org/teens/Pages/MACH/MACH1-Programs.aspx.

Santa Clara County Library District. 2017. "Teen Hackathon." November 11. Retrieved from https://sccl.evanced.info/signup/EventDetails?EventId=93563&ag=726&df=list&do=1&nd=60&lib=999&backTo=List&startDate=2017/11/11&endDate=2018/01/10.

Toronto Public Library. N.d. "Digital Information Hubs: Programs & Classes." Retrieved from http://www.torontopubliclibrary.ca/using-the-library/computer-services/innovation-spaces/programs-classes.jsp.

Getting Started

"A library takes the gift of reading one step further by offering personalized learning opportunities second to none, a powerful antidote to the isolation of the Web."

—JULIE ANDREWS (ALSC 1999)

Finding Facilitators

WHILE IT IS NOT AT ALL ESSENTIAL FOR LIBRARIANS to know how to code in order to plan and implement a coding program, it is certainly helpful. The good news is that there are many coding courses available online for little or no cost, ranging from beginner to advanced content. Here are some questions to help you evaluate if a coding course online is worthwhile:

- Is it self-paced?
- Does it provide options for both hacking prewritten code and writing code from scratch?
- Does it include explanations for the different symbols, words, or variables used?
- Does it teach why, and not just how?
- Does it provide explanations for errors instead of just correcting them?

Appendix D has a rubric for evaluating coding courses.

If a library is setting up a program for patrons to learn coding, it should be more than just sitting someone in front of a computer to participate in one of the many available online courses. In a small-group learning setting, there should be opportunities for collaboration, for shared problem solving, and for trying others' programs. That being said, the online courses are wonderful for filling gaps in understanding, for learning the basics, and for adding a new coding language onto an existing knowledge of coding. There is definitely a place for them in a library coding program, but it should not be the only component of that program.

MOST POPULAR FREE COURSES

- Code.org
- Khan Academy
- Google CS First
- Codecademy
- Coursera
- Udemy
- GitHub

MOST POPULAR PAID COURSES

- Pluralsight
- Lynda.com
- Code School
- Code Avengers
- Tech Rocket (offers some free courses as well)
- CS Education Online School

Supplement these courses with activities and projects that bring coding to life, either through on-screen animation or animation of an object like a robot or a vehicle. This gives purpose to the coding being learned. When a library or a school has the hardware needed for this type of project (STEM kits, circuitry kits, microcomputers, and recycled electronic parts), they can provide this opportunity for those who might not ever be able to have the option otherwise. Many libraries are putting together "coding crates" or "maker crates" available for circulation. Schools, clubs, small groups, and other organizations can then check these crates out and have temporary access to the materials needed to learn and apply a programming language.

Building a Collection

There are plenty of readily accessible online materials for use in a coding program; however, over time, as the popularity of the programs grow or as the library seeks to expand

Table 4.1. Subscriptions Available to Build a Collection

SUBSCRIPTION	TARGET USER	COST	CONTENTS
Bitsbox	Children 6–12 years	Around $20/month	Coding projects for young kids
MyStemBox	Girls 6–13 years	$25–30/month	STEM projects for girls
Creation Crate	Experienced coders ages 12+	Around $25/month	Arduino-based projects
MakeCrate	Experienced coders ages 13+	$30/month	Arduino-based projects
Robobox	Ages 14+	Around $30/month	Build-and-code" robots

the variety of offerings, they will want to gather a collection of materials and coding games. One of the easiest ways to keep your collection growing is with a subscription box. Each month the company will send you a box that contains a specific project, the instructions, and the materials you need to build it. A list of some of the most popular subscriptions appears in table 4.1.

Another great way to introduce equipment into a library coding programs is by purchasing basics kits offered for most equipment. Some, like the Arduino Basics Kit, provide circuit boards, accessories, and a book of project ideas that include instructions on how to code the projects. Others, like the Raspberry Pi Starter Kit, provide circuit boards, and the most commonly used accessories for beginner projects. Their web page offers an extensive library of projects using the materials in the starter kit. When purchasing materials, keep in mind that many companies offer bulk pricing, particularly for educators or for classes.

Partnering with the Community

Coding clubs and classes are a great opportunity to forge partnerships between public libraries and the community. Chances are that a very qualified facilitator can be found within your community—an older student or adult who has a good deal of experience and knowledge in computer science through schooling or as a hobbyist, or perhaps someone in a career field that involves some sort of programming.

Community members who work in STEM careers or programming hobbyists are also often willing to serve as mentors for young people in coding clubs or programs. This is a very impactful part of a coding program that involves young adults who are starting to be aware of career opportunities and potential fields of study in a secondary school setting. They also potentially bring an in-depth knowledge of coding that will be beneficial to more advanced coders participating in library programs.

Community partnerships could potentially be a great source for program funding as well. Often, local businesses seek ways to support local STEM programs. United States–based corporations often seek to sponsor and lead a team for robotics competitions or design clubs. They will provide materials and personnel for these events, and they are often hosted in public spaces like libraries. There are also many large-scale grant programs available from major companies that are looking for STEM projects to fund, and local branches of many businesses offer small grants or grant-matching programs to help purchase materials for programs.

One important community partnership is between the library and local schools. This opens opportunities for sharing materials, co-facilitating programs, and co-planning events. Many larger public libraries also serve their community by maintaining coding and makerspace equipment/tools that are able to be borrowed by schools.

PLANNING A CODING PROGRAM

Coaches, teachers, or facilitators
- Knowledgeable in whatever coding language is being used
- Motivating and inspiring
- Outgoing and friendly
- Connected to the library or to a contact person or liaison to coordinate with the logistics of the offering
- Ideally matched with participants at a ratio of one facilitator to five participants (more than one facilitator if you're looking at hosting younger kids)

Participants
- Determine what age and how many for the particular offering
- Unite around a specific interest

Curriculum
- What will they be learning or doing?
- On devices or unplugged?
- Challenge based or project based?
- Introduction to the language or a deep dive into it?

Venue
- Conference room, classroom, or shared public space (recreation center, for example)
- Easily accessible to participants
- Able to accommodate the demand on wireless or internet connection
- Large enough for expected number of participants
- Reasonable cost (if there is a cost, planners will need to determine who will cover that cost or if it will be shared by all participants)

Devices
- Provided? Or bring your own?
- Are there ports or outlets available to use for charging devices?
- Is there someone available on-site to help with technical issues?

Note: If participants are bringing their own devices, provide very specific information ahead of the offering, specifying what programs, apps, browsers, plug-ins, or operating systems will be needed. (Offer times ahead of the event to have participants bring in devices to check that they will work, if possible.)

When planning a coding course in a library setting, assume that you will get a mix of experience levels, but that you will likely be working with a lot of people with little or no background in coding. For that reason it makes sense to frame the course around learning the basics and then learning one or two of the more common languages. If you plan to offer a course that is specifically designed for beginners, for kids, for advanced coders, and so on, it is important to clearly communicate that in any publicity for the program, so you don't end up with patrons who are frustrated or bored.

CODING INTRODUCTORY COURSE: SAMPLE SIX-WEEK STRUCTURE

Week 1: What is coding? How does it work? Hands on—try a simple code on Scratch

Week 2: What can you do with coding? Dive in further with Scratch—loops, conditionals

Week 3: Use Scratch to run a project—MaKey MaKey, LEGO Robots, or Raspberry Pi

Week 4: Block coding versus text coding—try a simple code in Python

Week 5: Dive in further with Python—defining terms and variables

Week 6: Use Python to run a project—Raspberry Pi

Many libraries or schools don't feel ready to jump right in to hosting full courses. One-day codeathon events are a great way to expose the community to coding events, to get started offering coding opportunities, and to gauge interest among community members. A codeathon can be a competition among teams, a collaborative coding event, where everyone is working to come up with solutions to a common goal, or a chance to connect people across a distance to code together.

In 2015 a group of teachers in the United Nations International Schools in Asia organized a Global Codeathon event. They wanted to combine the teaching of coding with global collaboration in a way that the students found fun and meaningful. In the three years they have been hosting the event, it has grown to include schools from multiple countries. The event offers both a beginners coding and virtual meetup on the day of the event, as well as a competition for advanced coding teams leading up to the event. During the event, teams are working to create a program around a certain theme, to be shared at the conclusion of the event (Global Codeathon n.d.).

ONE DAY CODEATHON SAMPLE SCHEDULE

8:30–9:00 Introductions, objectives

9:00–10:00 Brainstorm and plan

10:00–12:00 Coding

12:00–1:00 Break, lunch

1:00–3:00 Coding

3:00–4:00 Sharing and presenting

One other format being used in libraries to introduce programming to both youth and adults at the same time is a "Teach Your Parents to Code" class. In this type of class, young people are asked to register with a parent or guardian and work together through a beginners coding program. One thing that makes this setup particularly appealing is that it is less intimidating for adults who have no coding background, since they will be working with their family member. At the same time, however, for both the adult and the youth, the act of going through the course together and helping each other understand will deepen both the understanding and the retention of the information.

Schools and libraries wanting to get started in offering coding programs need not feel that they have to dive straight in to offering a wide range of programs at multiple levels. Starting small with a short club or a one-day event is a great way to begin.

Key Points

- There are many different ways for librarians or volunteers to learn to code.
- There is no right or wrong way to set up a coding program.
- Programming could be anything from a one-day event to a multiweek course.

Resource

Global Codeathon—www.globalcodeathon.com
Bitsbox—https://bitsbox.com
StemBox—https://www.mystembox.com

References

Association for Library Service to Children (ALSC). 1999. "Libraries & Kids: Quotes You Can Use." November 30. Retrieved from http://www.ala.org/alsc/issuesadv/kidscampaign/kidsquotes.
Global Codeathon. N.d. Home page. Retrieved from http://globalcodeathon.com/.

CHAPTER 5

Teaching Coding to Young Children

IN THIS CHAPTER
▷ Is Any Age Too Young?
▷ Picture Books for Teaching Coding Concepts
▷ Toys that Teach Coding
▷ Coding Apps for Young Children
▷ Activity Ideas

"Whether we're fighting climate change or going to space, everything is moved forward by computers, and we don't have enough people who can code. Teaching young people to code early on can help build skills and confidence and energize the classroom with learning-by-doing opportunities. I learned how to fly a hot air balloon when I was 30,000 feet up and my life was in the balance: you can learn skills at any age but why wait when we can teach everyone to code now!"

—RICHARD BRANSON (CODE.ORG N.D.)

Is Any Age Too Young?

WHEN WE TALK ABOUT COMPUTER SCIENCE, most of us don't likely think of young children, but more and more we are finding out that the earlier children can be exposed to coding and programming concepts, the more they can grasp the more advanced programming ideas later. The biggest consideration when looking at coding programs for younger children is that they cannot be text laden. To engage and involve young learners, the program needs to be very visual. There are many options for that, which we will look at later in the chapter. Young learners also need to get immediate feedback to know how they performed on a task. Writing lines and lines of code and not seeing right away what the result is could result in frustration or lack of interest by younger children. Lastly, young children respond to characters, cute visuals, and sounds. Over the last few years, many coding activities and programs have emerged capitalizing on these things and helping reach young coders.

Although beginning coders are not likely to be designing elaborate programs, games, or web pages as a young child, it is important to lay the foundation for future learning in computer science. Much like learning a foreign language, the earlier they can start learning the conventions, symbols, and structure, the better. As a matter of fact, there are quite a few parallels between learning a programming language and learning to read or write. Early instruction in the basics of programming will help them understand what coding is and how it works. They need to understand how many things they do during the day have been assisted by something programmed with code. In the age of smartphones and tablets, it is increasingly easier to explain this to children, as they see how frequently these devices are used throughout the day. Lead a conversation about some of the things they encounter on a regular basis and start them thinking about how those things work:

- How does the computer know what to do when you click the mouse?
- Why do the arrow keys make the object on the screen go certain directions?
- How does the tablet know to open a specific app?
- How does the television turn on when a button is pushed on a remote control?

They're not going to know the answers to these questions, but they will begin to see that in order for these things to do what they expect them to do, someone had to write a program telling the device what to do. Then, while coding concepts are being applied through games or activities, they can begin to make the connection that they are learning how to control the computer or device as well.

> "What's most important to me is that young children start to develop a relationship with the computer where they feel they're in control. We don't want kids to see the computer as something where they just browse and click. We want them to see digital technologies as something they can use to express themselves."—Mitch Resnick (DevTech Research Group 2017)

As children grow as readers, they learn about cause-and-effect relationships, but even the very young can understand something like Simon Says, where they get a direction and have to follow it. This is a great way to introduce the idea of coding. They can begin to see and understand the need for clear and precise directions, a run command ("Simon says"), and a stop command ("Simon says stop"). Another great demonstration activity is Red Light–Green Light, in which the children know what action to perform when they hear specific words. This helps illustrate the idea that certain words are associated with certain actions, and that a command is always going to mean the same thing each time they hear it. This illustrates for them the concept of what a line of code is doing and begins to train their brain to think like a programmer.

There are many excellent ways to start our youngest children down the road of coding. If you go into an early childhood learning environment, you are not likely to see students sitting at rows of computers completing activities on a website. You are likely to see play-based interaction and learning. You are likely to see activities on the floor. You are likely to see conversation between the adults and the children about what they are doing and what it means. Young children should not be set in front of a computer and plugged into a program to learn how to code. They should be introduced to games and toys that apply coding within a fun and engaging activity. They should be programming toys, characters, or robots to move around the floor space, or to make a specific noise or color. This, along with conversation about why—the cause-and-effect of the program—will help young children start thinking like a coder. Much of basic coding is patterns and repeating sequences. Students as young as five years old have learned how to recognize patterns and make them repeat. Talking about these as loops and practicing making them repeat a designated number of times can be a first step in introducing and reinforcing this idea. And eventually children could work on "debugging" by analyzing the pattern and looking for places that the sequence is wrong in order to fix it—this can be done with beads, blocks, LEGOs, any types of small objects that they can arrange and rearrange.

IMPORTANT CONSIDERATIONS FOR CREATING CODING PROGRAMS FOR YOUNG CHILDREN

- Little or no text involved
- Engaging
- Visually stimulating
- Short duration
- Involves movement
- Mixes digital and unplugged
- Short instructions

When there are devices available, short turns on coding apps or sites are a good way to practice coding concepts. More and more options are being developed that make teaching coding with devices easier. When the Code.org website first became popular in the schools, young children were immediately drawn to it. Why? Because the levels involved the birds and pigs from Angry Birds, and the plants and zombies from Plants vs. Zombies—two apps that were very popular among school-age children. A few years later, Code.org had added many new activities to their Hour of Code collection, including a Disney's *Frozen* coding game and a *Star Wars* challenge. The users didn't know they were learning computer science—they thought they were playing a game about one of their favorite movies. If you look closely at the Code.org courses, you'll see why they, too, are popular among younger users—the introductory levels are picture based, little or no text, and provide immediate feedback.

Non-computer-based coding games are also becoming quite prevalent. These are often inexpensive and simple, great for teaching and reinforcing the idea of cause and effect. One of the things that is so appealing about coding toys or games is that they do not involve a device or a computer at all, so the concern of young kids spending too much time in front of a screen is removed from the equation. With so many device-free coding activities, even library and school programs with limited access to technology for young children can be teaching coding concepts. These are games and activities that reinforce the type of thinking introduced by a coding demonstration activity such as those mentioned earlier.

With younger children, activities need to be short and active. These children are not likely to sit still to listen to a long series of directions, nor can they commit multistep directions to memory. They need to be active, and they need to jump in to the actual task quickly, before they deem it boring. Many teachers of young children would tell you that the best way to do this is through the use of stations or centers. This structure keeps groups small, allows for a variety of different activities, and breaks up activities into short periods of time followed by movement. Depending on the size of the whole group, a coding club or class could have anywhere from three to eight stations. It's best to limit time at any one station to less than fifteen to twenty minutes, and limit the total time spent rotating through the stations to less than an hour (upper elementary and preteen children can sustain interest in these activities for longer and could handle rotating through stations for up to about an hour and a half). Best practice would be to alternate between a screen station, an unplugged simulation-type activity, and a coding toy or game, to keep kids engaged and break up time on the devices. Table 5.1 shows some options for setting up coding stations.

School-Wide Curriculum: Stratford Schools in Bay Area, California

The Stratford Schools include eighteen campuses in the greater San Francisco Bay Area of Northern California. The schools serve students from ages five to fourteen. They are well known for having the largest number of very young children participating in coding instruction—that number being over 1,900 students. The youngest students learn basic fundamentals using the Dash and Dot robots from Wonder Workshop and the various unplugged activities provided through the code.org courses, which center mostly on giving and following clear directions, provided through the Code.org courses.

Older children work through a mix of both unplugged and online activities in order to learn a variety of coding languages, like Scratch and Python. While they do work through some of the Code.org courses, their instruction is not entirely online and is not independent. They are being actively taught by a teacher rather than left on a device to figure it out alone. This is important when teaching coding to young kids, to be sure that they are not misunderstanding the information provided, and to offer coaching, give support, and answer questions. As the students move through the school's computer science program, they are adding on to the foundations they learned early on. Preteen students are securing their understanding of Scratch and Python, while also learning languages like Java and HTML. This knowledge is applied to building apps and creating games. Not only do these students have a very thorough and age-appropriate computer science

Table 5.1. Options for Setting up Coding Stations for Young Learners

SCREEN-BASED CODING	UNPLUGGED SIMULATIONS	CODING GAMES OR TOYS
Apps: Daisy the Dinosaur, Kodable, Light-Bot, Scratch, Jr. Site: Code.org Programming: Dash and Dot Ozobots	Binary Bracelets, Cracking Coded Messages, Building Patterns, Simon Says	CodeQuest, Bee-Bots, Code & Go Robot Mouse

education, but they are learning to apply it in a very real-life way by the end of their school time.

While this example is specific to a private school environment, it illustrates a very thorough scope of activities covering a wide range of ages. This could very easily be transferred to library coding clubs, with a beginners/young children's club starting out with the unplugged activities and games, the intermediate/school-age children's club starting to learn Scratch and Python mixed in with unplugged activities, and an advanced/preteen coding club could then focus on learning the languages used to create apps and games.

⊚ Picture Books for Teaching Coding Concepts

If You Give a . . . Books by Laura Numeroff

Good for: ages 4–10
Tips: These books are great for teaching conditional (If . . . then . . .) statements.

Hello Ruby Series by Linda Liukas

Good for: ages 3–10
Tips: Different books in the series teach parts of a computer, the Internet, coding, and virtual reality. The Hello Ruby section (listed in the resources at the end of this chapter) provides lesson and activity ideas to accompany the books.

If I Were a Wizard by Paul Hamilton

Good for: ages 6–12
Tips: This book teaches concepts like loops and algorithms.

Coding Palz Series by Liz Lah

Good for: ages 3–8
Tips: Titles like *Json's Password* and *Order, Order, Order* teach basic concepts of programming through the use of fun and engaging characters.

Usborne's Lift the Flap Computers and Coding Board Book

Good for: ages 3–10
Tips: This nonfiction book discusses how computers work. There are hundreds of flaps throughout the book to help readers see inside the computer and how it works.

⊚ Toys That Teach Coding

Think and Learn Code-a-Pillar by Fisher Price

Good for: ages 3–6
Tips: Children attach the body segments to the caterpillar's head in order to create a path for him to follow. To extend the learning for students who understand the basics, have

Figure 5.1. There are many games and toys coming into the market that teach coding fundamentals.

them try to code the caterpillar to reach a specific target. Expansion packs are available for purchase as well. Children can also simulate this activity with paper and pencil by using arrow cards to create the path.

Cubetto by Primo Toys

Good for: ages 3–8

Tips: Children control a wooden cube robot by placing command pieces onto the game board. Players will benefit from knowing the most basic idea that coding is a series of directions in a sequence. This will help them understand how what they are doing with the blocks and game board parallels writing code. Expansion kits are also available for purchase.

Robot Turtles

Good for: ages 4+

Literacy connection: Beep the Robot Turtle interactive eBook

Materials needed: Robot Turtles Game ($24.99 available online at http://www.robotturtles.com)

Prior knowledge/experience: Logo programming language, one of the first used widely in public schools for young kids, asked users to write commands to move a turtle around the screen, while drawing its path. This game pays tribute to Logo and the Logo Turtle.

Procedure: Players are drawing cards that show code-style instructions (turn right 90 degrees or move forward one step) to try to direct their turtle to the jewel in the middle of the board. Every player who gets a jewel is a winner.

Kibo Robots

Good for: ages 4–8

Materials needed: Kibo Robot and programming blocks, batteries

Prior knowledge/experience: It will help children connect this to computer science and programming if they have a basic idea of what code is—a sequence of directions to tell something what to do.

Tips: Users arrange the wooden programming blocks into the desired sequence, then scan the bar codes on the blocks with the Kibo scanner on the front of the robot. What makes this kit superior to others geared at the same age group is that it does include sensors, sound recorders, lights, and ways to decorate the robot so that children can personalize it and code it to do more than just move forward or backward. Using sensors introduces the idea of inputting information and triggering a reaction.

Code and Go Mouse Activity

Good for: ages 5–10

Materials needed: game set (mouse, green tiles, maze cards, hoops and purple blockades), batteries

Procedure: Players choose one of the maze cards and build the path shown. Then they program the directions to go through the maze into the mouse to reach the cheese (which is magnetic and will stick to the mouse's nose).

Tips: To simplify the activity for younger children, have them create their own maze and go through it. To challenge more experienced coders, you can extend the activity by asking them to go back through the path backward (pulling the cheese) in reverse.

Beebots

Good for: ages 4–8

Tips: Battery-operated bees can be programmed using the buttons on top. There are activities and curriculum available through the Beebots site; however, there are many

Figure 5.2. Beebots are one example of robots used to teach coding concepts to younger children.

possibilities for using Beebot to teach sequencing, problem solving, cause and effect, and estimation/prediction. Beebots can be purchased individually or as a "hive," allowing for more flexibility depending on budgets.

Dash and Dot Robots

Good for: ages 5–10
Tips: Dot is stationary; Dash moves around on wheels. Both can be programmed with a variety of apps. The Wonder Workshop website offers challenges, curriculum, directions for use, and everything you would need to get started using these with children. There are also accessory packs available for purchase, which allow for the robots to hold smartphones, connect to LEGOs, play the xylophone, and more. Dash and Dot are extremely engaging for school-age children.

Coding Apps for Young Children

Puzzlets: Cork the Volcano

Good for: ages 5–8
Tips: To use this game, you'll need Puzzlets game and pieces and the Cork the Volcano App. Through the app, children will be presented with the scenario, in which they are trying to help the three characters prevent the volcano from erupting. The player needs to

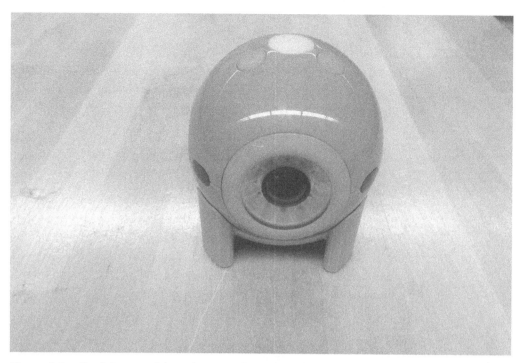

Figure 5.3. Dash is one of the robots produced by Wonder Workshop.

give the characters the directions to get them to the right places within the game. They give these directions by arranging and then scanning the game pieces. This is a game and app combination. Kids combine puzzle piece blocks to be read by the app and turned into instructions.

The Foos

Good for: ages 4–10
Tips: This program has three different types of activities—puzzles that require the player to program the solution to the puzzle, game creation activities, and mini-lessons to reinforce the concepts. This does require a $7.99/month subscription after a thirty-day free trial.

Cargo Bot

Good for: ages 5+
Tips: In this app, players are guiding a robot through the puzzle, moving crates and stacking them. This is a visual, drag-and-drop style of coding, making it great for early readers or non-English-speaking players.

Move the Turtle

Good for: ages 5+
Tips: While not necessary, it might be fun for users to know a bit of the history of Logo and the Turtle, as it relates to MIT and Mitch Resnick, to solidify the idea that what they are doing is not just an activity for kids.

Lightbot/Lightbot Jr

Good for: ages 6–12

Tips: This game asks players to move through a path while lighting up designated squares. It is a drag-and-drop app, which is easy for very young players. The levels get quite challenging eventually, making it applicable for older players as well.

Kodable

Good for: ages 7–12

Tips: Players guide various fuzzballs through mazes, trying to get all the gold coins without using too many blocks. The early levels of this app are drag-and-drop programming blocks, but more advanced levels actually graduate to text-based coding, asking players to look at lines of code and figure out what to add or change to make the fuzz do what they want it to do. Children love Kodable, and earning the new colored fuzz balls by passing certain levels is quite motivating to them!

Daisy the Dinosaur

Good for: ages 6–8

Tips: Daisy is a great starting-off point for young children to design their own programs. The app has two modes—tutorial and free play. In tutorial mode, the players are introduced to the different (text rather than pictorial) command blocks and walked through a series of tasks to demonstrate understanding of how to use and combine the blocks. In free-play mode, players can combine the same blocks they've already used to make Daisy do a variety of tasks. This is one of the few apps that doesn't tell users what they have to do, so it is a great chance for them to combine the commands in a sequence of their choosing.

Scratch Jr.

Good for: ages 6–12

Tips: Scratch Jr. can be adapted for many different levels of experience with coding. It's a great introduction for a class or club that will be moving on to Scratch or Blockly later. There are enough blocks and options to make it applicable for some more sophisticated coding projects, but it is also easy enough for nonreaders and inexperienced coders to get a feel for how visual programming languages work.

Code.org

Good for: ages 6+

Tips: There are two areas within the Code.org website that are useful with children. The first is the gallery of Hour of Code activities. These are highly engaging, as they incorporate characters with which most children are familiar—Disney characters, Flappy Bird, *Star Wars* characters, and Angry Birds, to name just a few. They are short and straightforward activities that are wonderful for applying coding and learning the basics.

For those wanting to go further, there are several series of courses, grouped by age. The K–5 courses, designed for ages five to eleven, cover a wide range of skills, starting with Level A, designed for nonreaders, through Level F, which gets into some fairly complicated game design coding. The sixth- through twelfth-grade courses, designed for ages nine to eighteen, provide everything from a condensed version of the K–5 courses to specifically targeted lessons for creating apps, games, or websites. The key, though, is not to sit a child in front of a computer and tell him or her to work through these lessons with no guidance. The facilitator or leader should be introducing and reviewing concepts as they are taught, discussing applications for the various concepts outside the world of the Code.org. Code.org offers teacher/leader/facilitator trainings to help those running programs feel comfortable working with young people on them.

◎ Activity Ideas

Beebot Map of the Community

Good for: ages 4–7
Literacy connection: The Beeman by Laurie Krebs
Materials needed: Beebots, coordinate grid (tape on carpet or on tarp)
Prior knowledge/experience: helpful to know basic directions—right/left
Procedure:
- Design a rough map of the community as a group, including major buildings and businesses, schools, main roads, and popular destinations.
- Lay out this map on a tarp, plastic sheet, or open carpet space.
- Give children a basic overview of how to program and run the Beebots.
- Have them practice "driving" the Bees through the map.
- Assign challenges to practice programming the bees through the map. These challenges can increase in complexity as the participants gain confidence with the programming.

Tips: With youngest users, it works best for kids to program in pairs, as working alone can be frustrating if they get stuck. Groups of more than two, however, do not give users enough time to program.

Other ideas with the Beebots could involve Battleship, treasure hunts, or demonstration of latitude and longitude.

Dash Maze

Good for: ages 6–10
Materials needed:
- Dash robots
- Device with Path or Go apps loaded
- Maze layout (made with blocks, tape, tables, or whatever creates boundaries or walls)

Prior knowledge/experience: It helps to know how to run the robot off of the Path or Go apps.
Procedure: Lay out the maze path, indicating where the start and finish are (it is fun to have one "beginner" path laid out first for the participants to drive through, then give them chances to make their own paths for each other).
Tips: For a deeper STEM connection, have them explore the angles, turns, and lengths within the maze.

Scratch Jr. Favorite Character Animation

Good for: ages 5–10
Literacy connection: any book with unique characters
Materials needed: variety of books, iPads with Scratch Jr. loaded
Prior knowledge/experience: none
Procedure:

- Have participants choose a book and look closely at the character.
- Teach the basics of Scratch Jr.—movement, costumes, changing backgrounds, changing characters, adding sound, and running programs.
- Give participants time and materials to plan out their character:
  - What would he say?
  - What would she look like?
  - How would he move?
  - Where would she be?
- Provide time to write the program to make their character come to life.

Tips: Host an event where children can share their animations with each other, with families, or with community members.

Key Points

- It is never too early to start children on the path of learning coding.
- There are many primary-geared games and toys available for helping young children learn the basics of coding.
- Block coding programs work best for younger users, since they are not as text rich.
- Engaging robots allow participants to apply coding to see immediate results.

Resources

Code.org—http://www.code.org. Free series of coding lessons appropriate for both young and older children
Code.org coding curriculum—https://code.org/curriculum/docs/k-5/complete.pdf
Cubetto by Primo Toys—http://www.primotoys.com
The Hello Ruby book series—http://www.helloruby.com/about
If I Were a Wizard by Paul Hamilton—https://www.wizardcodingbook.com/wizard-app
Scratch Jr.—http://www.scratchjr.com. Home site for iOS app that helps young children learn block coding

References

Code.org. N.d. "Leaders and Trend-Setters All Agree on One Thing." Retrieved from https://code.org/quotes.
DevTech Research Group. 2017. Home page. Retrieved from https://ase.tufts.edu/devtech/index.html.
Robot Turtles. N.d. Home page. Retrieved from http://www.robotturtles.com/.

CHAPTER 6

Teaching Coding to Older Children and Young Adults

"Whether you want to uncover the secrets of the universe, or you just want to pursue a career in the 21st century, basic computer programming is an essential skill to learn."

—STEPHEN HAWKING (CODE.ORG)

Why Do Young Adults Need to Know How to Code?

ANY READING YOU DO ABOUT COMPUTER SCIENCE and coding will mention careers and opportunities. Many employers are looking for candidates who know coding languages like Python, SQL, or Java. And these are the employers who have high-paying jobs to offer. We need to be sure our older children and young adults have the opportunity to compete for these jobs and the skills to make them qualified for these future positions. Young adulthood is often when people tend to develop programming as a hobby, as well. Many older children will likely at this point have a certain level of familiarity with the beginning coding programs, so they are looking for something more challenging and more versatile. They want to get more involved with coding for robotics, for controlling drones, for building websites and apps, or for learning about hacking (not all hacking is bad!).

The focus of coding instruction with older learners is more on understanding how things work. Rather than just coding for the sake of learning to code, your older learners are going to want to code to create something or control something. The language taught to older coders really depends on what they want to do with it. If they're specifically wanting to build a computer using an Arduino board, for example, then they will need to learn the Arduino coding language.

One of the biggest challenges that libraries and schools face in teaching older learners how to code is that they may have a very wide range of prior experience and understanding of coding languages. While many are likely to have had similar exposure in school, those who have been involved in robotics or who code as a hobby may have a much broader knowledge of different languages. It is not essential for librarians, teachers, or facilitators to know all of the coding languages, but they should certainly know how to find them, and be comfortable with some basic debugging/troubleshooting to support more advanced learners.

ⓖ Where Will They Use Coding?

Robotics

Whether as part of a formal robotics competition team or just a fan of the many types of robots on the market currently, to use and control a robot or drone, they need to understand how to program them. Most of the more common robots and drones use drag-and-drop block programming, like Scratch, Blockly, or Tickle. Many robotics activities involve a pair or a group of people working together to solve a challenge, which not only teaches coding skills, but teamwork, collaboration, negotiation, problem solving, and communication.

Website Building

You may have heard the recent term *kidpreneurs*, referring to young adults who are starting successful businesses with products they make or create and market for sale. While these young entrepreneurs could certainly host their goods on a large public site, they would benefit from having a unique site, where they could include more information, more photos, and personal elements to help increase sales. In an academic setting, a website is a great way to create a portfolio of work to showcase a person's growth over time and draw emphasis to their talents. Many employers or secondary schools no longer look for resumes and standard applications but look at portfolios of applicants. Thirty years ago, patrons went to the public libraries to use the typewriters and computers to fill out applications and print them. While that is no longer necessary, now they need access to the tools (both knowledge and equipment) to develop their professional portfolios.

There is a lot of higher-level programming that goes into security and back-end functions on a web page (those things that are not visible to the page's visitor, but make

Figure 6.1. Block coding uses colored blocks that can be dragged together to create a series of commands.

it function properly). Most programming that would be taking place in a library setting would focus on content management, and those things that the visitor would see or use when going to that page. This might involve any one of several different languages, depending on the purpose of the page and the type of contents involved. Those looking to learn web development languages to prepare for a career in this field will likely be more prepared for the job market if they are familiar with and/or proficient in more than one of these languages.

Some of the preprogrammed website building platforms, like Google Sites, Weebly, and Wix, allow users to drag and drop content into their web page, which adds prewritten code into the source code for their site. This makes website design accessible to very young users as well as beginners having little or no knowledge of web development languages. Even when using these, however, it is helpful to have some understanding of the syntax of code, for the purpose of troubleshooting. When something isn't working the way it is supposed to on the page, it is often because some small line of code did not delete when something was edited or changed on the page. Knowing how to click over to the code for that page and identify the problem can help solve it much more quickly.

As previously mentioned, many of the older learners of development languages are doing so to create a website for a small business or to build a professional portfolio for potential employers. Some of the emphasis in courses or clubs designed for these learners should be geared toward learning what makes a good web page (aesthetics, layout of pages and subpages, compatibility with browsers, and media contents, among other things). It saves much time and confusion in the long run to have these users design the outline of the page on paper before trying to translate it to the computer.

SAMPLE STRUCTURE OF WEB DESIGN COURSE FOR YOUNG ADULTS AND ADULTS

- Brainstorm qualities of a good web page
- Learn the basics of web development languages
- Plan a web page on paper
- Design and program the home page
- Design and program the subpages
- Preview and test
- Publish

```
<table border="1" bordercolor="#888" cellspacing="0" style="border-collapse:collapse;border-color:rgb(136,136,136);border-width:1px">

<tbody>

<tr>

<td style="width:496px;height:294px"><font color="#000000" size="6"><u>Topic</u></font><br>

<font size="5">Using Google Earth create a tour (Lit Trip) highlighting key locations from a historical fiction novel.</font></td>

<td style="width:520px;height:294px"><span style="background-color:rgb(255,255,0)"><br>

<img
src="https://www.google.com/chart?chc=sites&amp;cht=d&amp;chdp=sites&amp;chl=%5B%5BGoogle+
Gadget'%3D20'f%5Cv'a%5C%3D0'10'%3D199'0'dim'%5Cbox1'b%5CF6F6F6'fC%5CF6F6F6'eC%5C0'sk'%5C
%5B%22Include+gadget+(iframe)%22'%5D'a%5CV%5C%3D12'f%5C%5DV%5Cta%5C%3D10'%3D0'%3D20
0'%3D264'dim'%5C%3D10'%3D10'%3D200'%3D264'vdim'%5Cbox1'b%5Cva%5CF6F6F6'fC%5CC8C8C8'eC
%5C'a%5C%5Do%5CLauto'f%5C&amp;sig=Pn1Y7zZt73j8iv476Rm37UmXwpE" data-
igsrc="http://101.gmodules.com/ig/ifr?mid=101&amp;synd=trogedit&amp;url=http%3A%2F%2Fhosting
```

Figure 6.2. HTML is one of many coding languages commonly learned by many programmers. *Courtesy of Cleverism*

Community Outreach

When teens and adults are learning something new, they need to see the purpose and application for it. There is not much relevance to designing a website with no actual goal of publishing and using it. Therefore, development courses or programs will be much more meaningful if there is a purpose to the website they are building. Some of the members may come into the course with an idea already in mind of what they want to build, and why. There might also be participants who want to know how to build websites, but don't have a particular one in mind at the time. There are many opportunities for public libraries to partner with members of the community in website development programs.

There may be nonprofit organizations, clubs, groups, or new businesses in the community looking for help with designing and launching a website. When a group is growing past the stage of being new and just getting off the ground, they might be ready to publicize their mission, their contact information, or their events. This would be a perfect opportunity to partner in creating the site at little or no cost to the group in question.

There may also be entrepreneurs in the area who would like help in creating a web page to showcase their goods. There are host sites like Etsy that are very commonly used, but as artists grow their businesses, they may want to also grow their online presence, but lack the knowledge of how to do this, and in fact they may also lack the desire to learn how to do it themselves. Pairing a coding program member with an entrepreneur needing a website can create a partnership that is mutually beneficial.

For younger adults, teenagers, and possibly even older school-age children, meaningful web development can be paired with a sense of community and awareness by having them create a website to bring attention to a local or regional problem and solicit ideas for solutions. This might be an environmental problem, a social problem, or a community infrastructure problem. For example, a group in Wisconsin was concerned about a lack of public recycling in their community. They created a web page outlining the concern, including photos of some of the recyclable items in the garbage and the local landfills, and linked to research sites. Their subpages focused on updates as discussions about the problem advanced, highlighting some of the proposed solutions. They publicized this site through local schools and community businesses to draw attention to the problem. While a perfect solution has not yet been found, they learned a great deal about how to best design their website to communicate their concerns most clearly and efficiently.

Tinkering

A growing number of teens and young adults are taking up tinkering as a hobby. In particular, building robots, drones, and computers is becoming a common pastime. This wouldn't necessarily require coding, however to be able to use what they build, these hobbyists need to know coding to run their creation. Many hobbyists like to share their creations at public events like Maker Faires, which are occurring in an increasing number of cities around the world. To be able to program their product to do what they'd like not only gives their design more purpose, but it creates a bigger impact on those seeing it at the Maker Faire, knowing that someone like them built it and wrote the program to control it.

One activity that is growing in popularity across the United States is a one-day upcycling event. Participants take old electronic devices, everything from rotary dial phones to DVD players, and deconstruct them, salvaging parts they want to use to build something new. Then they combine these parts with various recycled materials—plastics, cardboard, containers, or whatever might be around—to build something new. They then program it for a specific function. These events can be theme-based, where everyone is designing something around a specific question, challenge, or problem; or they can be open-ended, where the participants choose what they will create and what it will do.

Game/App Creation

In December 2017 there was another story in the US news about a pre-teenager (in this case an eleven year old) who saw a problem and created an app to help solve it. She was trying to figure out a way to help with the contaminated water problem in Flint, Michigan. She invented an app that can test for contaminants in the water more quickly, using a microprocessor, sensors, and an iPad, expediting the process that would help thousands of people. We want our young people to be good global citizens, helping solve problems that plague cultures around the world. This is a wonderful example of how coding makes this possible.

But young adults are also creating apps for entertainment—the market for game apps is extremely active, and young adults make up a big portion of the designers who are building these apps. The games are sometimes quite simple, sometimes very complex, and often end up being big hits. Libraries hosting app creation clubs are finding them to be very popular and very successful.

> Recently my son became obsessed with playing Plants vs. Zombies. He has played many levels and variations of the game. During one conversation about the game, he explained one of the "never-ending" levels of the game, followed by, "I wonder how they program it to be never-ending." This led to a conversation about loops and stop commands. I could watch his mind thinking through all of this and wanting to test it out. Kids and young adults want to understand the "how" behind the games they are playing.

There are learning programs being used often in schools to deliver content in the form of a game. Some of the more commonly used ones are Gamestar Mechanic and Quest Atlantis. As an avatar in the game, the player completes activities that teach or reinforce information about a variety of subjects, such as math, geography, science, and grammar. These are relevant outside of a school setting as well. Families who homeschool their children or young adults looking to learn something new or expand their knowledge of a topic would like to be made aware of these game programs, and possibly even be provided with the materials, the training, or the coaching while going through them. Other similar game programs teach users how to write code to create their own game while playing in the program. These are extremely popular in schools, since they allow for players of many levels to all learn new skills within the same program. The benefit of activities like this is that it is easy to see the results of the programming immediately, to assess the accuracy of the code that was written.

WHAT MAKES A GOOD GAME?

- Engaging graphics that don't distract
- Plot
- Interesting characters and scenes
- Levels to advance with progress
- Clear and straightforward directions
- Multiple possible ways to win or lose
- Interesting name and premise

⊚ Programs for Coding with Older Learners

Alice Storytelling

Good for: ages 10+

Tips: In this program, users are writing code in Java. By completing activities along the way, they are putting together components of the storyline. This is an engaging and accessible program for beginners to text-based coding.

Game Maker Studio

Good for: ages 12+

Tips: This program utilizes a drag-and-drop method, similar to block coding programs, but with more complex options. One limitation is that the program is primarily for 2D games and not 3D games.

Sploder

Good for: ages 10+

Tips: Sploder allows users to create games using one of their five gaming templates. The community is popular among younger game designers, and it has some security measures in place, but for the most part, the community is monitored by a team of members.

Bloxels

Good for: ages 8+

Tips: The Bloxels kit includes a plastic tray and dozens of multicolored cubes, each of which represents something specific (an object or an action) within the Bloxels app. It is possible to use the app without having the kit, but with younger users, the kit is a great way to really instill an understanding of the coding element.

Roblox

Good for: ages 8+

Tips: Roblox is an interactive, multiplayer community where users can play games made by others, as well as design and code their own games to post in the community. One thing that makes Roblox such a good tool with younger users is the attention to security and privacy, particularly for those users under thirteen years old.

Scratch

Good for: any age user who can read fairly well

Tips: The Scratch website features a lot of already made games for users to play and/or hack to personalize. There are also many tutorials available at all levels. Scratch offers add-on extensions to make the code compatible with popular circuit kits, like Little Bits and LEGO WeDo kits.

Minecraft Edu

Good for: ages 7+

Tips: Most anyone who has spent time around younger kids in the last few years has heard of Minecraft. It is a world in which players create structures, gather resources, and fight off zombies. Minecraft and Microsoft partnered to create a version of Minecraft that teaches coding. There is a mini-version on the Code.org website, as well as extensive curriculum in the Minecraft Edu platform.

Books about Coding for Young Adults

Coding Bugs and Fixes (Kids Get Coding) by Heather Lyons

Good for: ages 12+

Tips: It is important to not just teach how to write code, but how to troubleshoot as well. This is a great way to reinforce that.

Computational Fairy Tales by Jeremy Kubica

Good for: ages 10+

Tips: This is a fun way to integrate computer science with familiar stories.

The Byte-Sized World of Technology by Melvin and Gilda Berger

Good for: ages 8+

Tips: This book of technology facts is a great way to reinforce how many places in life use coding.

The Way Things Work Now by David Macaulay

Good for: ages 10+

Tips: The book's predecessor, *The Way Things Work*, has been a favorite for years. This version looks into updated technologies as well, keeping it relevant.

Coding Music

In recent years, the integration of coding with music composition has become more popular among younger programmers. Programs and accessories make it possible for users to create tones and rhythms using their computers. There are options, like Scratch, that make this process simple enough for even younger children to understand, and there are more complicated options—like Sonic Pi, music coding in Python—that are more appropriate for older or more experienced programmers. Compared side-by-side, reading music and reading code are actually not that different; they don't have much meaning to someone not familiar with what the different symbols and sequences represent, but once you know what they mean, you can understand what you're looking at clearly. Similarly, writing music and writing code are actually not that different either. Once programmers

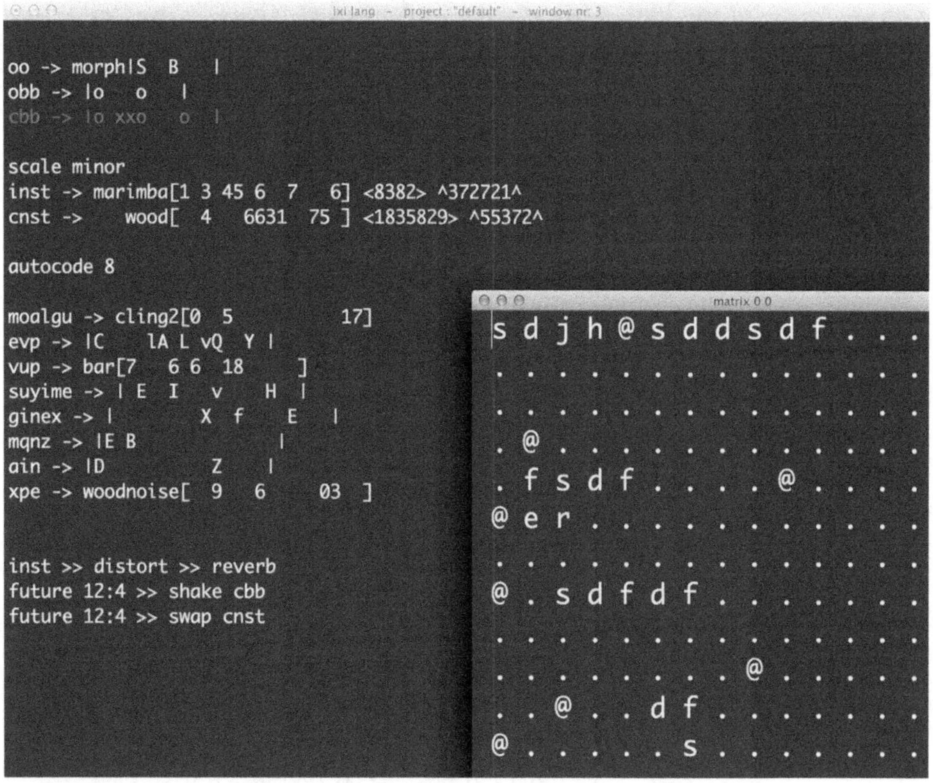

Figure 6.3. Coding music is increasingly becoming popular as programs integrate computer science with music. *Courtesy of Wikipedia*

know the language-specific terms, symbols, or sequences, putting them together in a pattern results in music.

The Raspberry Pi microcomputer, which is covered in more detail in chapter 8, has become one piece of equipment that is used with Sonic Pi frequently for coding music. Pimoroni, a company that, among other things, manufactures and sells add-ons (called hats) for the Raspberry Pi microcomputer, has created a piano hat and a drum hat that simplify the process of creating music with Python and the Raspberry Pi. By following certain structures within the code, music can be produced quite easily.

Block coding programs such as Tynker and Scratch include sound blocks that can be manipulated to sound like certain instruments, to play specific notes, and to hold those notes for desired lengths. Blocks of code can be written to play simultaneously, allowing for multiple instruments or multiple notes to be played together. Coders as young as nine or ten years old have successfully created Scratch Symphonies by programming a song into their code and then having multiple instruments play it together, accompanied with a programmed drum beat. This is how the MaKey MaKey board can be used to play such music as well. A simple Internet search of MaKey MaKey piano, guitar, or drum will provide links to programs that other users have created and shared in Scratch or another similar program, so that when a MaKey MaKey is connected, the instrument is played.

The Dash Robot also comes with an accessory for music. A xylophone and a mallet can be snapped on to the robot, then users can write code in an app called Xylo to program Dash to play a song.

A program called Ear Sketch offers free online courses in coding through music. The program includes both music concepts and computer science concepts, with coding in the Python and JavaScript languages. This is a wonderful way to not only blend the two ideas but also provide some context for programming for those who are musically inclined. Young adults who are proficient at reading and/or writing music would likely love learning how to write more intricate music without needing anything more than a computer. This can open doors for creative expression and possibly even a future career.

Ⓖ Activity ideas

Promotional Website for Library Event

Good for: ages 12+
Materials needed: computers, examples of promotional websites
Prior knowledge/experience: understanding of what promoting an event involves, basic understanding of coding (the specific language depends on what platform they will be using to create the website)
Procedure:
  • Give participants a write-up of the pertinent details about an upcoming event (either in the library, at a local school, or in the community)
  • Teach the basics of the particular language/platform they will be using
  • Discuss what makes a good website
  • Use a planning template to lay out structure of pages for the website
  • Build the pages, starting with the home page
  • Preview and debug
  • Publish
Tips: Post links to the promotional sites on the library home page. Have designers leave a space to upload photos and videos after the event.

Animated Holiday Cards

Good for: all ages
Materials needed: iPads or computers with Scratch bookmarked or opened
Prior knowledge/experience: none
Procedure:
  • Teach the basics of Scratch—movement, costumes, changing backgrounds, sound, and looping.
  • Show them where to find specifically relevant sprites for that holiday (optional).
  • Give participants time to plan out their greeting card.
  • Provide plenty of time to complete coding and check for problems.
  • Help participants email the cards to their recipients if that's what you plan for them to do.
  • Younger children will ask if they can print their cards. You will need to explain to them that when they are printed, they are no longer animated.
Tips: Plan ahead—how will they share their cards? Will they bring the recipient in at the end of the session, or will they be emailing them to a recipient (if so, specify that they will need to bring an email address with them when they arrive). If you want participants to save their animations, they will need to create an account using a personal email address. Plan ahead and ask them to be ready to sign up for an account.

Animated Art (Spirographs)

Good for: ages 10+

Materials needed: computers with Scratch bookmarked or opened

Prior knowledge/experience: basic understanding of angles and measuring them; intermediate level understanding of Scratch

Procedure:

- Briefly discuss or review angles, paying particular attention to angles less than 90 degrees
- Show or remind participants about the following tools in Scratch:
  - Draw function
  - Change pen color
  - Turning sprite in a specific angle
  - Looping
- Give time to write code
- Provide time to test and change code after it is written (encourage participants to play with different sized angles, different colors, different speeds, or different pen widths)
- Share art with the group

Tips: If the group is having trouble picturing what the project will look like, have some examples ready to show them. It would be wonderful to host these projects in some sort of digital gallery, either on the library website or with devices on display.

Extension option: For those who are particularly skilled coders, challenge them to re-create this activity using a text-based coding language

Mini-Maker Faire

Good for: all ages

Literacy connection: Rosie Revere, Engineer

Materials needed: iPads or computers with a variety of coding programs available, various circuitry materials, electronics parts, and recycled goods

Prior knowledge/experience: depends on the scale of the project the participant wants to create

Prior to the event:

- An event of this type requires a good deal of promotion and advertising ahead of time. Recruit participants and volunteers from local high schools or technical schools.
- Solicit donations of old electronics, recyclable materials, and consumables such as duct tape, batteries, tools, and hardware.
- Determine in advance and clearly communicate whether participants should come with something already built, or whether they can build at the library during the event or during established times prior to the faire.
- Ask exhibitors to RSVP prior to the date of the faire to help with planning of space, tables, chairs, and electrical sources.

Procedure:

- Set up a large area in which the exhibitors will display their creations (it helps to assign specific spaces to allow for those who have specific needs like electricity, access to water, access to sunlight, or larger amounts of space, to get what they need).

- Allow for an hour or more prior to the start of the event for exhibitors to set up and test their creations.
- Allow for several hours of "open to the public" time for the faire.
- Encourage attendees to take information about coding and/or sign up for future courses and programs.

Tips: Reach out to local secondary schools, science and technology businesses, and members of the community. Including participants from different places may create partnerships for future activities and provide contacts of potential mentors or volunteers.

Note: During the 2017 Milwaukee Maker Faire, in Milwaukee, Wisconsin, a free mini-conference for librarians and educators was held in one part of the facility. Organizers brought in educators and librarians who had experience with coding, making, tinkering, and organizing public STEM events to sit on a panel and field questions about how to get similar programs started in other schools and libraries around the region. Libraries hosting mini–Maker Faires could offer similar opportunities as part of the event, reaching out to neighboring libraries and area schools to send attendees and panelists to speak about the roles coding and making play in the lives of our youth.

Gameathon

Good for: all ages
Materials needed: iPads or computers with internet access
Prior knowledge/experience: none
Procedure:
- Provide a brief overview of several game building platforms such as Scratch, Sploder, Roblox, and Minecraft.
- Discuss the components of a good video game.
- Provide planning templates for participants to think through their project.
- Give ample time to build, test, and improve games (this might be an all-day activity).
- Give participants a time to share their game with the group or with the public, as well as to play the other participants' games.

Tips: After giving an overview of some of the platforms, it may work best to divide the workspace into "stations" so that programmers using the same platform are all located together, allowing for conversation and collaboration about their projects as they build. Consider partnering with another organization somewhere else to allow for sharing on a more global level.

⊚ Key Points

- As programmers become older or more proficient, they need to understand the purpose for the code they're writing.
- There are many reasons for wanting to learn coding.
- Web design is a great way to help participants learn coding at the same time as learning a valuable skill for career readiness.
- Many proficient coders get involved in app or game design as a way to share their coding with others.

⊚ Resources

Ear Sketch—http://www.earsketch.com. Coding music site

Scratch—http://www.scratch.mit.edu

Sonic Pi—http://sonic-pi.net/files/articles/Live-Coding-Education.pdf. Tutorial on how to use Sonic Pi

Stencyl—http://www.stencyl.com/. Online game making site

⊚ References

Cleverism. 2015. "Top Programming Languages used in Web Development." June 21. Retrieved from https://www.cleverism.com/programming-languages-web-development/.

Code.org. N.d. "Leaders and Trend-Setters All Agree on One Thing." Retrieved from https://code.org/quotes.

Coding Unplugged

Low-Tech Options

"Often computer science is taught using programming first, but not every student finds this motivating, and it can be a significant barrier to getting into the really interesting ideas in computer science."

—FROM *CS UNPLUGGED*, BY TIM BELL, IAN H. WITTEN, AND MIKE FELLOWS (2015)

WHETHER YOU'RE TALKING ABOUT a public library, a school classroom, or an individual wanting to integrate coding, one of the most common barriers is lack of access to technology. This does not need to stand in the way of teaching the fundamentals of coding. There are many activities that are very helpful in introducing coding structures. Many kindergarten classrooms are using these activities as a way to begin building the foundation for teaching coding with computers later.

With your very youngest children, trying to teach an introduction to programming by putting them directly in front of a computer will actually cause more headache and chaos than learning. These children are likely not independent or confident enough on the computer to know what to do without a helper. This also brings up, again, the reliance on text for many of the computer-based applications, which also becomes a barrier for younger learners.

"Unplugged" coding activities can be as simple as songs, call-and-answer activities, large-group games, or movement activities. While there are also many toys and board games available to enforce these concepts, many of those work better with smaller groups, pairs, or even with individuals, and programs offered in a public library or school setting don't want to exclude eager participants by limiting the numbers too much. Offering an unplugged coding club would be a fun, active, age-appropriate option for early school-age children, and expanding that offering to be a mommy/daddy and me type club would make it possible for even younger children to take part.

⑥ Teaching the Fundamentals

When you think about it, coding is based off of the general idea of getting a command, processing that command, and doing what you were told. Dozens of children's games involve this same idea. Engaging younger children in an activity where they have to listen to a command and complete a task starts building that connection needed to write conditional statements in more advanced programming as they get older.

One of the most important blocks, or commands, in a series of lines of code is ironically the one that gets overlooked often when teaching coding to children. That is your start, or run, command. Use activities and games to emphasize this action—think about anything that involves a phrase along the lines of "Start when you hear me say go." Simon Says is a great example of this. Players receive a specific command about what action they are supposed to perform, but they need to listen for their start command "Simon Says . . ."

I remember many games in my physical education classes as a child that involved listening for my number, and when my number was called, I had to run in and get the ball, or try to be the first to the cone, or whatever the objective was. By listening for my number before starting to move, I was waiting for that start command. Although I didn't know it at the time, this was a great way to reinforce the idea of a run or start command in writing a computer program.

Many games that are already probably sitting on shelves of many homes, schools, libraries, and toy stores can be used to teach some of these concepts. If they are going to be used to develop an understanding of coding, however, it is going to be important to include conversation explicitly pointing out the connection to programming and introducing programming vocabulary into the activity. This is often as simple as calling it a command instead of an instruction or referring to their "run command" instead of calling it "saying go."

⑥ Activity Ideas for Teaching the Fundamentals of Coding

Using Codes

Codes Study—Morse Code, Binary Code, Ozobot Code

Good for: ages 8+
Materials needed:
- Printed translators for various codes
- Paper
- Markers or Pencils

Procedure:
- Discuss some of the more common codes that people use.
- Practice translating words or letters into several different codes.
- Discuss how the code for the Ozobot is different than the other codes (that the code is a certain pattern of colors rather than shapes or letters).
- Practice controlling the Ozobot with color codes.

Tips: Teach students how to calibrate the Ozobots using a dark black circle before you begin. This will save frustration later.

Secret Messages

Good for: any age
Materials needed:
- Paper
- Writing materials
- Code ciphers for any code to be used

Procedure: Have participants write messages in code and exchange them to translate.

Coding Cards

Good for: any age
Materials needed:
- Several cards featuring arrows and numbers

Procedure: Use papers or cards with arrows on them to create instructions for a partner.

Robot Cup Stacking

Good for: ages 6+
Materials needed:
- Cards with drawings of different cup-stack formations on them
- Plastic cups
- Paper
- Pencils

Procedure:
- Put participants into pairs or groups.
- Choose one person to be the "robot" and one to be the programmer.
- Have the programmer choose a challenge card but not show it to the robot.

- The programmer needs to write the code to direct the robot to replicate the stack using left, right, up, and down arrows.
- The programmer may not say anything to the robot—the robot reads the code off of the paper and follows it to build the cup stack.
- When the robot is finished stacking, compare the cup stack with the picture on the card.

Tips: Practice the movements for each arrow as a group before you begin the activity, so that everyone understands them the same way.

If . . . Then . . . Group Games

Engage the group in any games that require listening for a certain cue or watching for a signal in order to start the action. Discuss the start command and the stop command, and the conditionals (If _____ then _____).

Red Rover

Good for: age 6+ (large group needed)
Materials needed: none
Procedure:
- Divide the group into two teams.
- Have each team line up across from each other, about twenty or more feet apart, holding hands in a chain.
- On their turn, one team chants "Red Rover, Red Rover, let _____ come over" naming one of the other team's players.
- Once they hear their name, that player runs over to the other team.
- If the player is able to break the chain of the other team, he goes back to his team and brings a player from the opposing team with him to join his team.
- If the player is unable to break the chain of the other team, he joins that team.
- The goal is to end the game with the largest team.

Red Light–Green Light

Good for: ages 3 and older (two or more players needed)
Materials needed: none
Procedure:
- Choose one player to be "It."
- That player stands at the end of the play area with her back turned to the rest of the group, who are standing at the start area.
- The player who is It says "green light" with her back still turned, and when she says green light, the other players run as far toward her as they can.
- When the player who is It says "red light," she turns around, and the other players have to freeze.
- If the one who is It catches any players still moving once she turns around, those players are out.
- The goal is to be the last one left in the game.

Giving Verbal Coding Commands

Discuss the need to be accurate and specific when writing code. An optional conversation would be about efficiency of the commands (for example, rather than "walk two steps forward," then "walk four steps forward," combine that into one command of "walk six steps forward").

Trust Walk/Blind Treasure Hunt

Good for: ages 10+
Materials:
- Large space without obstructions
- Blindfold

Procedure:
- One player is blindfolded.
- The other player(s) give(s) commands about what direction that player is to turn and how many steps to move.
- Their commands should be limited to the following:
  - Run
  - Stop
  - Turn left
  - Turn right
  - Move _____ steps forward
  - Move _____ steps backward
- The commands should lead the blindfolded player to a "treasure," through a maze, or across a designated space.

Extension opportunity: For older children, introduce the idea of turns in 90-degree increments rather than just turning right or left.

Integrated Literature Activities to Teach Coding

Many favorite children's stories involve moving through a path or a trail. Using a table top mat or a floor mat with the places from the story drawn or labeled on them, children can write the symbols of the code to re-create the path that the character traveled. A few examples of favorite stories that would work well for this are the following:

- *The Gingerbread Man*
- *Going on a Bear Hunt*
- *The Very Hungry Caterpillar*
- *The Three Billy Goats Gruff*

Another version of this activity could have children acting out the character's travels themselves on a larger floor mat or moving from one labeled area in the room to the next.

Large-Group Activities to Teach the Structure of Code

When you have a larger group gathered to learn about coding, it works well to do a simulation activity. The following are the most important ideas to emphasize:

- Variables—what symbols or terms represent in the code
- Conditionals—If . . . then . . . statements
- Actions—move, turn, jump, play a sound, pick something up (the more specific the better to emphasize the need to be precise in their code)
- Loops—differentiate between "repeat," "repeat ___ times," and "repeat until ____"

Human Loop

Good for: ages 5+

Materials needed: papers with miscellaneous action words printed on them: run, stop, repeat, if, then, repeat ____ times, repeat until ____, and any actions you want to include

Procedure:

- Give the first person in the line the word *run* and the last person in the line the word *stop*; then distribute the action words only among the other people in the line.
- Demonstrate that after the person with the *run* sign holds it up, the remaining people go down the line sequentially doing whatever their action word says, until they get to the person who holds up the *stop* sign (see table 7.1).
- Next switch out the *stop* sign for a *repeat* sign.
- Repeat the activity, with everyone doing whatever their action word says in succession, over and over to illustrate the impact of the *repeat* sign (see table 7.2).
- Next switch out the *repeat* sign for one of the other two repeat signs, and either designate how many times they should repeat, or tell them to repeat until you raise your hands.
- Repeat the activity. Discuss how when they are coding, they need to be clear about how many times to repeat a sequence to achieve a desired result.
- Then, introduce the *if* and *then* . . . by putting them after the *run* sign (see table 7.3).

Table 7.1.

run	beep	buzz	snap	beep	clap	buzz	snap	clap	beep	clap	stop

Table 7.2.

run	beep	buzz	snap	beep	clap	buzz	snap	clap	beep	clap	repeat
beep	buzz	snap	beep	clap	buzz	snap	clap	beep	clap	beep	buzz
snap	beep	clap	buzz	snap	clap	beep	clap				

Table 7.3.

run	if *beep*	then *buzz*	snap	buzz *(stays silent)*	clap	buzz *(stays silent)*	snap	clap	beep	buzz *(makes noise)*	stop

Tips: Don't rush this activity—stop frequently along the way to discuss what these signs are doing within the sequence.

Teaching the Structure of Code through Music

There are many parallels between music and code. In chapter 6 we talked about the similarities between reading both music and code and writing both music and code. More similarities can be found beyond that. In music, you need to identify the time signature and the key signature to be able to correctly interpret the melody of the song. Similarly, in coding you need to identify the variables before being able to correctly interpret the function of the code. And of course, lines of code are repeated in loops, just like lines of music can be repeated with the presence of a repeat sign. For those who are quite experienced in reading music, similarities can be drawn between music with codas or fines, and code that has conditionals or *repeat until* commands. It is very logical that the two are merging quite seamlessly to lead to teaching coding through music instruction.

To introduce the idea of patterns and loops, rhythm and percussion instruments would be very helpful. Kids can each take an instrument and play it in turn, with *repeats*, *If . . . then . . .* statements, and *run/stop* commands mixed in. And participants can take turns being the "conductor" to give the *run* and *stop* commands.

MIT has developed curriculum for teaching music and Logo coding program simultaneously, as they complement each other quite well. Renaissance Art Academy in Los Angeles, California, has students writing songs about coding to help reinforce the concepts for other students.

Teaching the Structure of Code through Art

> "I think that great programming is not all that dissimilar to great art. Once you start thinking in concepts of programming it makes you a better person . . . as does learning a foreign language, as does learning math, as does learning how to read."—Jack Dorsey (Code.org n.d.)

Many children have experience with color by numbers and paint by numbers. This can be directly connected to the idea of coding—if you see a certain number, then you draw in a certain color. Activities as simple, and as time-tested as these are laying the foundations for coding. Stick Together Products has created a project that applies the paint-by-number idea in a larger group setting. Their Stick Together Mosaic Posters apply a letter code to various colors of stickers. By placing the square stickers in the correct spots on the mat, participants reveal a hidden picture. This activity is as relevant for adults as it is for children, using a code to reveal a desired outcome (Demco 2017).

One of the most popular connections between art and coding is through knitting. Where coding is, at its most basic, binary—0 and 1—knitting is, at its most basic, also binary—knit and purl. This lends itself to many parallels between the two. If you look at the written directions for knitting a particular pattern, it actually looks quite similar to lines of code.

Figure 7.1. Stick Together Community Murals by Demco are a way to integrate coding and art.

Many feel that teaching coding through connections outside of computer science (like music or art) helps reinforce the idea that it is important to learn programming regardless of what field they're likely to go into, rather than computer science being a topic in isolation. It is also a way to connect girls with coding, which continues to be an area that needs focus, as we'll discuss in the next chapter. Drawing connections between a new, and possibly intimidating topic like programming, and something that is familiar and accessible, is a really important way to reach those who would not otherwise consider coding as something they should know how to do.

⊚ Activity Idea for Teaching the Structure of Code through Art

Plan a Voyage

Good for: ages 7+

Materials needed: maps, either real or fictional

Prior Experience Needed: none

Procedure: This activity could be done as a road trip plan, a tour of the community, or a voyage around the world. Participants designate a starting point, and then they write the code for where the voyage takes them. If desired, maps could be overlaid with grids to establish an arbitrary unit, or older participants could use units such as miles or kilometers to describe how far up, right, left, or down to travel.

Extension option: Participants could pair up and trade codes to see if they accurately represented the voyage they really wanted to take.

⊚ Teaching Coding through Toys and Games

By their very nature, many games, both old and new, teach and reinforce coding concepts. They have cause-and-effect relationships, they rely on conditionals for particular turns or moves, and they often use repeating patterns and universal symbols. Here are some in particular that come to mind:

Chess: The role of each piece in being able to move a certain direction and number of steps can be connected with variables and constraints in lines of code.

Simon: Listening and repeating patterns reinforces the idea of exact patterns and repetitions.

Twister: If I spin a certain command, *then* you need to find a way to put that appendage on that color. By drawing players' attention to that conditional relationship, they are more aware of how many times in their days they are fulfilling "If . . . then . . ." commands.

Other games are designed to explicitly teach coding concepts.

Code Mouse Maze: Players pull a challenge card and build the path indicated on the card. Then they program the battery-operated "mouse" to travel the path and retrieve the cheese.

Code Monkey Island: Monkeys move through a path, responding to specific actions from the cards that are drawn on each turn.

Robot Turtles: Combining a story with a board game, players have to choose which path to follow based on the situations presented in the story. Not only are they engaged in practicing If . . . then . . . conditional relationships, but they have to evaluate the efficiency and value of different options before choosing them.

Ozobots: Participants draw paths on paper for their Ozobot to follow, including particular color patterns that tell the Ozobot to perform certain actions, like speed up, turn right, pause, or change color.

⊚ Offering an Unplugged Coding Event

Depending on the target age of the participants, a course teaching the fundamentals of coding without computers could be a one day "camp" or a multi week course. The most effective way to do it would be to start with large-group activities, then progress to small-group or individual activities. Being that most of these small-group activities can be run simultaneously, it would most likely work best to set up stations or centers, which could be themed as a journey around the world with different ports, a road rally with pit stops, or a Coding Olympics with different events. What is going to be important is presenting many different activities that reinforce the fundamental concepts, so that participants can more easily apply them to different applications, and to include conversation and repetition of the important terms and concepts that will be carried over into coding.

⊚ Activity Ideas for an Unplugged Coding Event

Crack the Code

Good for: ages 5+ (able to read)

Literacy connection: Top Secret Code Book by Dan Newman

Materials needed: code cipher that translates letters into something: other letters, colors, numbers, symbols, etc.

Prior knowledge/experience: basic understanding of how to encrypt or decipher a message in code

Procedure: Provide written messages that are encrypted into code. Using the cipher that they have been provided, participants decipher the message.

Tips: Multiple messages could be sequenced together as a scavenger hunt as well.

Table 7.4.

a	b	c	d	e	f	g	h	i	j	k	...
z	y	x	w	v	u	t	s	r	q	p	...

Coded Jewelry

Good for: ages 5+

Literacy connection: If You Give a . . . series by Laura Numeroff

Materials needed:
- Yarn
- Beading wire or pipe cleaners
- Multicolored beads, many of each available color

Prior knowledge/experience: This is a great way to introduce the idea of patterns and loops in coding. Basic knowledge of patterns is helpful, but not imperative.

Procedure:
- Have kids craft patterns out of the beads.
- Discuss how these are like the repeating patterns, or loops, that we use in coding to make the same thing happen multiple times.
- String the beads onto the wire or yarn to make bracelets or necklaces.

Character	Binary Code	Character	Binary Code	Character	Binary Code	Character	Binary Code	Character	Binary Code
A	01000001	Q	01010001	g	01100111	w	01110111	-	00101101
B	01000010	R	01010010	h	01101000	x	01111000	.	00101110
C	01000011	S	01010011	i	01101001	y	01111001	/	00101111
D	01000100	T	01010100	j	01101010	z	01111010	0	00110000
E	01000101	U	01010101	k	01101011	!	00100001	1	00110001
F	01000110	V	01010110	l	01101100	"	00100010	2	00110010
G	01000111	W	01010111	m	01101101	#	00100011	3	00110011
H	01001000	X	01011000	n	01101110	$	00100100	4	00110100
I	01001001	Y	01011001	o	01101111	%	00100101	5	00110101
J	01001010	Z	01011010	p	01110000	&	00100110	6	00110110
K	01001011	a	01100001	q	01110001	'	00100111	7	00110111
L	01001100	b	01100010	r	01110010	(	00101000	8	00111000
M	01001101	c	01100011	s	01110011	)	00101001	9	00111001
N	01001110	d	01100100	t	01110100	*	00101010	?	00111111
O	01001111	e	01100101	u	01110101	+	00101011	@	01000000
P	01010000	f	01100110	v	01110110	,	00101100	_	01011111

Figure 7.2. Binary code table. *Courtesy of CS Unplugged, www.csunplugged.org*

Extension options: Assign specific commands to different colors of beads (e.g., red means turn right, blue means forward one step, green means turn left, etc.). Then have kids create a series of commands to try out with a partner.

Adaptation for older children: Introduce the idea of binary code and how computers use and translate binary code. Distribute code sheets that translate letters into binary. Use black and white beads only, and have the children build their names out of binary sequences using the black and white beads. Assign the white beads to represent the 0 and the black beads to represent the 1, or vice versa. Extra room on the yarn or wire can be filled with other colored beads, leaving the black and white sequences to be the focal point. Letter sequences can also be divided by adding smaller beads, or clear beads between them.

Key Points

- To teach the basic ideas of coding, a device is not necessary.
- There are many small- and large-group activities that reinforce key components of code.
- Many of the games we have in our houses and schools, and have played many times, apply coding fundamentals.

Resources

CS Unplugged—https://cs-unplugged.appspot.com/en-gb/. Creative Commons activities and integration ideas for teaching computer science without a computer

Computer Science Field Guide—http://csfieldguide.org.nz/en/index.html. Activities for teaching computer science without a computer, appropriate for high school and young adults

References

Bell, Tim, Ian Witten, and Mike Fellows. 2015. *CS Unplugged: An Enrichment and Extension Program for Primary-Aged Students*. Retrieved from http://csunplugged.org/wp-content/uploads/2015/03/CSUnplugged_OS_2015_v3.1.pdf.

Code.org. N.d. "Leaders and Trend-Setters All Agree on One Thing." Retrieved from https://code.org/quotes.

Demco. 2017. StickTogether Tiger Mosaic Sticker Poster. Retrieved from https://www.demco.com/products/Upstart-Promotions/Posters-Décor/General/StickTogether-Tiger-Mosaic-Sticker-Poster/_/A-B00384914.

Korbey, Holly. 2013. "Can Learning to Knit Help Learning to Code?" MindShift, October 8. Retrieved from https://www.kged.org/mindshift/31684/can-learning-to-knit-help-learning-to-code.

Integrating Coding with Making

"Tell me and I forget, teach me and I may remember, involve me and I learn."

—CHINESE PROVERB

ALL AROUND US, in community spaces, schools, and libraries, makerspaces (sometimes called hackerspaces, tinkerspaces, creation labs, design labs, and idea labs) are coming into use. These spaces, which combine design thinking, creativity, technology, and innovation in one space, have brought technology that was previously not common outside of the computer science field into the hands of children, young adults, casual users, and technology hobbyists. The rise in popularity of makerspaces has made tangible applications of coding—driving robots, programming microprocessors, automating creations, and integrating art and technology—relevant and accessible for people of all ages. It has also made it more important and more urgent that librarians, teachers, and makerspace facilitators learn and understand coding themselves.

As participants design projects or use new equipment, they can control and automate parts of it through coding. These spaces often contain equipment, kits, and robots that can be controlled using visual programming languages. Some are designed for those with more computer science experience, or at least a bit more exposure to various coding programs and languages. Some, however, are simple and engaging enough for children as young as four or five years old to learn and use. Enter any makerspace and you're likely to see or hear about some of the equipment in this chapter.

"Even short exposure to robotics can have a lasting impact on students to pursue complex careers that they may have never considered."—Laura Ziegler, EdD (2016)

Traditionally, the word *robotics* has conjured images of complex, large robots with very advanced skills, designed and programmed to perform certain tasks. But with the recent introduction of several popular toy-like robots into the makerspace market, some of the emphasis has shifted away from building the robot to adapting it for certain tasks and to writing the program to control it. And with that shift, robotics are being incorporated into activities and clubs for much younger children and a much broader audience. Users analyze the steps and functions necessary to create an action that they desire and write the program to communicate that to whatever robot they're using. Some of the most popular robots in makerspaces have the ability to be modified in a variety of ways with add-ons and accessories, making them very versatile, fun, and engaging.

Sphero

One such robot series is the Sphero series of bots. The original Sphero was developed in 2010 as a toy for the purpose of connected play—play in a virtual world. Ross Ingram, a developer of Sphero robots, defines it this way: "Connected Play is the connection with humans our robots enable" (Ingram 2015). The goal was to integrate robotics and play. In the years since, the company has created several other models of Sphero as well as a variety of accessories, such as various ramps and covers, to extend the uses of Spheros for learning purposes. Within the first year of Spheros being on the market, over a dozen different Sphero-compatible apps were developed and released, both by the Sphero company and by independent developers. While some involve very little actual coding and function more like a joystick, many, like Lightning Lab and Sphero App, use block-dragging coding to control the Sphero.

Dash and Dot

Another very popular set of robots is the one made by Wonder Workshop—Dash and Dot.

These durable, entertaining robots immediately draw young users in with their bright colors, fun shapes, and silly voices. Dash and Dot come with attachments and accessories that allow them to be compatible with LEGOs; to play the xylophone; and to carry, hold, push, and drag things. There are five different apps developed by Wonder Workshop that can be used with Dash and Dot, as can several other apps designed to control more than one device, like Tickle (which we looked at in an earlier chapter). The Blockly app uses block-dragging coding to program the robots. Dash and Dot are definitely aimed to a younger audience than Sphero, so they are a great introduction to robotics, and in the style of traditional school robotics programs, Wonder Workshop runs a Dash and Dot Robotics Contest annually, in which entrants are given the task of programming their

Figure 8.1. Dash and Dot robots are engaging for younger children.

Dash to perform certain tasks. The most creative and successful entrants are awarded prizes. The Wonder Workshop website also offers an extensive collection of lesson ideas and resources for teachers, club leaders, and facilitators, making the integration of Dash and Dot into a library, school, or makerspace program quite easy.

Drones

Drones have recently entered the public market, immediately surging in popularity as they allowed users to take their coding somewhere completely new—into the air. Additionally, they are highly engaging and have many possible applications. Drones are not without their downsides, though. The price tag can be high, and it is important for users to understand the safety and liability that comes with using them in schools and libraries—and to teach and model appropriate and legal use. Drones are run on microcontrollers, which need to be programmed in order to function. So by telling the drone where to go and what to do, students are learning and demonstrating mastery of programming.

One of the more popular drones for use with children and young adults is the Parrot Drone, out of France. Parrot offers rolling and flying drones that can be controlled through Tynker or Tickle, making them easy to use with school-age children as well as adults. The drones are designed with users learning coding in mind, so the company's website also provides activity ideas and very thorough directions.

Activity Ideas for Coding with Robots

Art-Bots

Good for: ages 5–12

Literacy connection: The Squiggle by Carole Lexa Schaefer

Materials needed:

- Robot that can move in lines or curves—Dash, Sphero, Rolling Parrot Drone, or others
- Drawing device—marker works best
- Paper
- Rubber bands
- Duct tape
- Device for programming (tablet or computer)

Prior knowledge/experience: basics of programming using a block-based programming language (e.g., Blockly, Tickle, Sphero)

Procedure:

- Attach a crayon or marker to the robot using rubber bands or duct tape (the tip of the marker or crayon should be touching the drawing surface).
- Write the program for whatever drawn object is desired.
- Test and adjust as needed.

Tips:

- Have the user draw or sketch the drawing first, writing notes about which way to turn, how far to move forward, and how many degrees to turn, if applicable.
- Start with regular polygons—squares, rectangles, triangles—before attempting designs with many different sides, curves, or angles.

Robot Mazes/Obstacle Course

Good for: ages 8–16

Literacy connection: Labyrinth by Louise Gikow

Materials needed:

- Robot such as Dash or Sphero
- Painter's tape
- Device to drive the Robot (tablet or computer)

Prior knowledge/experience:

- Basic understanding of programming language being used to drive the robot (Blockly, Tickle, Scratch, or Tynker, for example)
- Understanding of directions, angles, and estimated measurements

Procedure:

- Create a course for the user to follow by making a path of tape on the ground.
- If desired, add obstacles, such as tunnels made from chairs, blockades, or walls to be avoided.
- Write the program to navigate the maze.
- Test and adjust as needed.

Tips: To practice navigating the maze, young children can use a driving app, such as Go for Dash or Sphero Drive to work on controlling the robot, even though there is no programming involved.

Bot-fest

Good for: ages 10 and older

Literacy connection: Awesome Dawson by Chris Gall

Materials needed:

- One robot per event or challenge (if only one robot is available, users can take turns)
- Duct tape or masking tape
- Kebab skewers
- Balloons
- Small cardboard box
- Dowel rods
- String
- Small lightweight ball
- Devices for driving robots (tablets or computers)

Prior knowledge/experience:

- Basic knowledge of the programming app being used
- Minimal background knowledge about jousting, chariot racing, polo, and bocce ball

Procedure:

- Robot "Jousting"
  - Attach the kebab skewers to the robot, pointing in one direction. (If you are using a Sphero, you will need to create a "belt" of some kind out of cardboard, paper, 3D printing to which this will be attached.)
  - Attach the inflated balloon on a wall or a box.
  - Competitors will write code to drive their robots toward each other, trying to direct the skewer at the opponent's balloon. The first one to pop the opponent's balloon wins.
  - Alternate 1: Balloons can be attached to the robot on the opposite side of the skewer, and robots can drive toward each other trying to pop the balloon—this works better with driving apps like Go for Dash and Sphero Drive for Sphero, rather than writing code.
  - Alternate 2: Either of the aforementioned methods can be followed with drones, adding the challenge of "driving" the drone through the air to try to pop the opponent's balloon.
- Chariot Racing
  - Attach the small cardboard box to the robot using string, tape, rubber bands, or whatever materials (I like to have racers each design their own chariot).
  - Design a course for the racers to follow using painter's tape on the floor or creating walls with blocks or something similar.
  - Write code to direct the chariot through the route.
  - Test and alter as needed.
- Robot Soccer Shoot Out
  - Attach dowel rods to the side of the robot so that the end of the dowel rod is grazing the ground.
  - Create a "goal" out of a cardboard box or tape lines against a wall.
  - Write the code to try and "kick" the ball into the goal by knocking the ball with the dowel rod.
  - The first robot to three points wins.

- Sphero Bocce Ball
  - Toss the lightweight ball away from the robots' starting point to act as the marker.
  - At each person's turn, they code the Sphero (using the Sphero block-coding app) to try to get as close to the marker as possible.
  - The person who comes closest gets the point.
  - Then the marker is rethrown and code is rewritten.

Tips:
- The activity could be turned into a Bot Olympics for an Olympic-themed activity.
- These games can be adapted to work with a variety of robots and apps.

Sphero—Dot Day

Good for: all ages

Literacy connection: The Dot by Peter H. Reynolds

Materials needed:
- Spheros
- Variety of creation materials and art/craft supplies (paper, tape, cardboard, cloth, ribbons)

Prior knowledge/experience:
- Familiarity with International Dot Day
- Read the book *The Dot* as a class before this activity

Procedure:
- After reading the book *The Dot*, introduce International Dot Day (see the resources section for the website).
- Users plan what they're going to turn their Dot (Sphero) into.
- Using any of the materials provided, they turn their Sphero into something.
- Have a Dot Parade in which the users write the code to move their Dots through a parade route to share their designs with others.

Tips:
- Plan how the Sphero will still be able to move inside of their design.
- Dot Robots (from Wonder Workshop) work well for this activity, too—instead of coding for movement, users would be coding for sound or lights.

Specific Robotics Competitions

Good for: ages 8+ (depending on the complexity of the specific robot and coding program)

Literacy connection: Awesome Dawson by Chris Gall

Materials needed:
- Challenge cards specifying a task for the robots to complete
- Robots
- Device for programming robots (tablet or computer)
- Materials specific to a challenge

Prior knowledge/experience: basics of specific programming language being used

Procedure:
- Teams of students receive a challenge card that gives them instructions about a specific task they need to program their robot to complete.

- Alternative 1: Teams all receive the same challenge card and are looking for different ways to complete the task. Points can be awarded on success, creativity, and so on.
- Alternative 2: Teams are given a time limit in which to complete their task.

Tips:
- Take a few minutes to discuss ideas before they start coding.
- Keep teams small to ensure that all members are getting experience writing the code.

Vehicle Making

Create a shell or cover for the bot that turns it into a specific type of vehicle.

Good for: ages 5+

Literacy connection: If I Built a Car by Chris Van Dusen

Materials needed:
- Robots that can move or travel (Parrot Drones, Spheros, Dash)
- Various building materials
- Wheels and axles

Prior knowledge/experience:
- Understanding of wheels and axles
- Basics of the programming language being used

Procedure:
- Users create a cover or shell for their robot to turn it into a vehicle—car, boat, train, truck, and so on.
- Users program the robot to move like that vehicle (slow vs. fast, straight line vs. curves).

Tips: With certain programming apps, like Blockly for Dash, you can also write code to play certain sounds, so users would be able to make their vehicle look *and* sound like the real thing.

Robot Battleship

Good for: ages 8+

Materials needed:
- Coordinate grid—could be drawn on paper, projected from high-mounted projector, created with tiles or tape on the floor
- Paper copies of the coordinate grid
- Robots
- Devices on which to control the robots

Prior knowledge/experience: how to read a coordinate grid

Procedure:
- Each player sets the color of their robot to be something different than the others so robots can be easily distinguished.
- Before play begins, each player places his battleships on the paper coordinate grid—the number and size of the ships can be agreed upon by the players, anywhere from one to six ships, ranging in size from two squares long to five squares long. They draw their battleships on their paper and make sure they know the coordinates for each one.

- On his or her turn, the player "attacks" a battleship by coding her bot to drive to a square on the large coordinate grid.
- When the robot lands on the square, the player being attacked has to determine if the robot "hit" one of his ships or not. He declares hit or miss.
- The players each make some sort of mark on their paper coordinate grid to remember which squares have been hit for future turns.
- If every part of a battleship has been hit by the robot, the player being attacked announces that ship to be sunk.
- The winner is the first one to sink all of the opponent's ships.

Tips:

- For younger children, use a single quadrant coordinate grid.
- For older players, use a four-quadrant coordinate grid to make the game more challenging.

⑥ LEGO Robotics

LEGOs are not new to us, but they are increasingly present in the world of STEM and STEAM (science, technology, engineering, arts, mathematics). The development of LEGO Education and the robotics kits tied in with the popularity of the Logo programming language out of MIT in the 1980s. At that time, the LEGO company was starting to develop brick kits that included pneumatics and motors, when their attention was drawn to the work on the Logo programming language becoming so common with young users. Developers in the LEGO corporation and at MIT were both already exploring similarities between the work being done around learning through hands on and play based activities, and the potential for using LEGOs as a learning tool. Both groups wanted to see LEGO and Logo work together (Watters 2015). Where young users were becoming familiar with moving the Logo turtle through writing a series of commands, developers wanted to create an opportunity for children to design their own robot to control—not just a turtle. This led to the first LEGO Robotics programmable kits. The evolution over the last forty years of the kits available has allowed for something for users with all levels of experience.

WeDo

The WeDo kit is the LEGO company's entry-level robotics kit. It is designed for younger users or those new to the idea of programming LEGO creations. The programming software is a block-dragging interface similar to Scratch. There are extensive instruction books with ideas for building, but there are enough different pieces, connectors, gears, and motors to build a variety of creations without instructions, too. The one restriction is that the WeDo brick that runs the motors needs to be tethered to a computer to receive the signal.

Mindstorms

LEGO Mindstorms offers users a programmable brick, eliminating the need to be connected to the computer. Programs can be written on the computer and uploaded to the brick or programmed directly into the brick. Its popularity was boosted by the start of

LEGO League, a Mindstorms robotics club that sponsors annual challenge contests for LEGO robotics clubs.

Tetrix

Wanting to develop something even more advanced, LEGO combined with Pitsco, Inc., to develop Tetrix Robotics. Materials are compatible with Mindstorms but are more versatile, since the pieces are larger, metal, and connect with bolts. Like Mindstorms, Tetrix Robots are used in annual First Robotics competitions, primarily in middle schools and high schools, and are usually a prominent feature at Maker Faires.

Activity Ideas for Coding with LEGO Robotics

Animate a Character

Good for: ages 6–12
Literacy connection: any book with distinctive characters
Materials needed:
- LEGOs
- WeDo motor and controlling brick
- LEGO WeDo software or Scratch software (requires additional extensions to be activated to work with WeDo controllers)
- Computer

Prior knowledge/experience: basic knowledge of how to program in the WeDo software
Procedure:
- Participants build the character, making sure the parts that will be animated can move if needed.
- While building, they need to be sure to build the motor into the character's design in a way that the motor is stabilized so it doesn't just spin and tangle up the cord.
- Once the character is finished, the builder should attach the motor to the controlling brick and plug the brick into the USB port on the computer.
- Before programming, it is important to launch the WeDo software and check in the menu that it has recognized the motor that is connected.
- Participants will program the WeDo motor to move when the program is started.

Tips:
- Start with a sketch and a plan for how the motors will fit into the build.
- The design for the character needs to take into account that there is a cord running from the motor to the brick, and another tethering the brick to the computer.

Robotics Challenges

Good for: ages 12+
Literacy connection: House of Robots by James Patterson
Materials needed:
- Age-appropriate LEGO Robotics building kit
- Controller brick and appropriate cords to connect to the computer
- Miscellaneous materials specific to the challenge task
- Challenge cards outlining tasks for the teams to complete

Prior knowledge/experience:
- Knowledge of how to program the brick using the appropriate software
- Knowledge of how to upload programs to the brick using the USB cord (Mindstorms and Tetrix)

Procedure:
- Teams of students receive a challenge card that gives them instructions about a specific task they need to program their robot to complete.
- Alternative 1: Teams all receive the same challenge card and are looking for different ways to complete the task. Points can be awarded on success, creativity, and so on.
- Alternative 2: Teams are given a time limit in which to complete their task.

Tips:
- Take a few minutes to discuss ideas before they start coding.
- Keep teams small to ensure that all members are getting experience writing the code.

Create an Automated Model of a City or Community

Good for: ages 6+

Literacy connection: Block City by Robert Louis Stevenson

Materials needed:
- LEGOs
- Base plates
- LEGO WeDo motors and controller brick
- Computer

Prior knowledge/experience: very basic knowledge of what the WeDo motors can do

Procedure:
- As a group or team, builders should plan what their LEGO community will contain.
- Within their plan, they need to identify what parts can be automated with motors (tilt, spin, or sensors/sound).
- Once the community has been built, the team needs to attach the motors to the controller brick and plug the brick into the computer.
- When the WeDo programming software is launched, it is important to check in the menu that the computer is sensing all motors attached.
- Builders write the program to automate features of their community (make a car roll down the street, open a door on a building, sense movement and play a screeching brake sound, etc.).

Tips: Have users play with controlling more than one WeDo motor at a time through the computer program so that they understand which blocks to use to get the desired result.

⊚ Programmable Microcontrollers

A very popular item in makerspaces, and with electronics and circuitry enthusiasts, is the microcontroller (also called a microprocessor and microcomputer). This is essentially a minicomputer, with various plugs, pins, and slots for things like SD cards, attaching monitors, attaching sensors, and a range of output devices. We have had microcontrollers for years, in kitchen appliances, fitness equipment, toys, and games. Part of what makes them so versatile is that they are small, relatively inexpensive, and reprogrammable. Because of this, they can be used for a large number of projects, from building a photo booth, to creating a motion sensor. With many brands and styles of microcontrollers available, it might be difficult to figure out where to get started. Fortunately the Internet is full of recommendations, write-ups, project ideas, tutorials, and guides.

Microcontrollers can be confusing for those with limited computer programming experience, particularly because the programming software is typically not a graphical (block-dragging) format (although program languages like ArduBlock for Arduino have created that option); instead, it is a language like C or BASIC. With an understanding of how these, or similar languages work, it becomes very easy to adapt and write code, as well as to troubleshoot when a program isn't working. Once the microcontroller and its particular programming language become familiar, a world of possibilities opens up.

MaKey MaKey

Of all of the options available, this is the best to use with younger children. It is engaging and provides a high level of success in a very short amount of time. The front side of the board is designed to replace certain keys on the computer keyboard when the circuit is closed. The board can be used immediately with preprogrammed activities on the Internet, such as the MaKey MaKey piano, drum set, or Pac-Man game. Or it can be programmed for more advanced functions by using coding programs like Tynker or Scratch. One of the more popular applications of this among younger users is programming everyday objects to play sounds or music by attaching wires from the board to conductive materials, so that when two materials are touched, the circuit is closed and the sound plays. When the back side of the board is used, it acts more like an Arduino board, where various input and output devices can be attached to expand the possibilities.

Raspberry Pi

The Raspberry Pi microcontroller is a very affordable and versatile option. It is designed to perform the same functions as a larger computer, but running off of a pocket-sized board. The board has several USB ports, an HDMI port, ethernet port, and more. A Raspberry Pi can be programmed with several programming languages, including Scratch, Java, and Python. This makes it a very desirable board because it's very easy to learn programming with it. Another wonderful thing about the Raspberry Pi is that on the company's website, there are links to training opportunities for teachers, librarians, or casual users, both online and face to face. Additionally there is an entire curriculum (Raspberry Pi n.d.) with activity ideas, making it very easy to integrate into a coding or making program. There are many accessories for sale to complement the Raspberry Pi, such as cameras, sensors, and LED matrices, making it extremely versatile for dozens of projects appropriate for users just starting out, as well as experienced coders and tinkerers.

Arduino

Another very common microprocessor is the Arduino. As makerspaces became more mainstream, this was one of the more popular items on the market, so they are commonly found in school and library makerspaces. The applications of Arduino boards are numer-

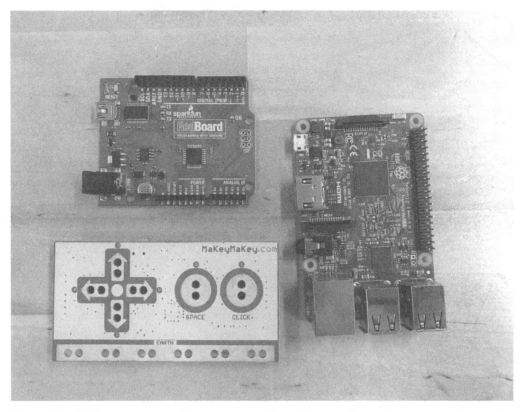

Figure 8.2. Microprocessors allow more experienced coders to apply programming to devices they design or invent.

ous. They can be used, much like a Raspberry Pi, to automate functions, apply sensors, run various output devices, and control peripheral devices, like robots or machines.

Ardunios can be run off of a software program called Arduino, which is text based, as well as a block-programming version called ArduBlock. The choice between text and block languages for programming makes them more accessible to users of various ages. Subscription kits like Creation Crates send kits that contain Arduino boards with accessories needed to use them in fun and engaging projects.

Creation Kits

Alongside of the hardware that is needed for coding with microprocessors, there are also many kits being introduced to the market that allow users to build robots, computers, and any number of other creations that will then be powered by these microprocessors. One example is the Hummingbird Kit, which uses Arduino boards to power robots the user creates. Kano Kits provide the peripheral devices needed to turn the Raspberry Pi microcomputer into a working PC. And the Little Bits Arduino Coding Kit creates a bridge between a circuitry kit like Little Bits and an Arduino board.

Activities using the microprocessors often involve some sort of button or sensor that triggers the run command for the program. Where and how this is applied is dependent on the type of project being created. Sensors available for these boards range from light and sound sensors to humidity and temperature sensors, making their practical applications numerous. The most meaningful way to apply understanding of how to use and program the microprocessors is to analyze a real-life problem—in their lives, in the community, or in the world—and design something to help solve that problem. It need not be terribly complicated, but regardless of what the design is, the application of the coding to something that young people could use in their lives makes it meaningful and memorable.

The popularity of makerspaces is bound to continue growing. In order to move from simple creations to more elaborate inventions, coding should become a regular component. Not to mention that learning to code so that you can control something you invented is a powerful and meaningful way to get started in programming.

◎ Key Points

- Makerspaces are often a part of public library programming.
- Many of the activities in a makerspace, including robotics, require coding to run.
- Learning to program a microprocessor opens up a great number of options for what to create and build.

◎ Resources

Arduino—http://www.arduino.cc
International Dot Day—http://www.thedotclub.org/dotday/get-started
LEGO Robotics—https://www.lego.com/en-us/mindstorms
MaKey MaKey—http://www.makeymakey.com
Raspberry Pi—http://www.raspberrypi.org
TETRIX Robotics—https://www.tetrixrobotics.com/
Wonder Workshop—https://www.makewonder.com/apps

◎ References

Ingram, Ross, 2015. "What Is Connected Play." Medium, September 29. Retrieved from https://medium.com/@rossingram/what-is-connected-play-50d0804b8574.
Raspberry Pi. N.d. "Curriculum." Retrieved from https://www.raspberrypi.org/curriculum/.
Watters, Audrey. 2015. "LEGO Mindstorms: A History of Educational Robots." Hack Education, April 10. Retrieved from http://hackeducation.com/2015/04/10/mindstorms.
Ziegler, Laura. 2016. "Drones in Education." *Tech & Learning* (blog), April 21. Retrieved from http://www.techlearning.com/blogentry/10614.

Reaching Out through Coding

"Learning to code is a fantastic opportunity equalizer—if you're good at it, it can help you achieve your dreams."

—SENATOR CORY BOOKER (CODE.ORG N.D.)

Reaching Underrepresented Populations

WHETHER YOU'RE LOOKING at coding from the viewpoint of a technology corporation, a public library, or a school, you will find that most proponents are in agreement that all youth need to be exposed to computer programming early in their lives, and consistently throughout their youth. It is the responsibility of public schools, libraries, clubs such as the Boys and Girls Club, and other national organizations to offer these opportunities to all youth, regardless of their age, gender, school history, primary language, and academic ability.

After spending a little time teaching programming, however, you will find that it is truly accessible to all, regardless of any of the aforementioned classifications. The biggest barriers are access to devices and access to written language. Both of these hurdles can be overcome fairly easily with publicly run coding clubs or programs.

Coding clubs offered in a public school or library can be introductory clubs, geared toward those who have absolutely no history with programming, or those who have spent years learning the foundations and are ready to take their knowledge further. These clubs, however, do not need to be limited to one experience level or the other. Partnering novice coders with experienced coders to participate in challenge activities provides an opportunity to grow both in their understanding of the fundamentals and how to apply them.

It is important to reiterate that organizers and sponsors of these types of clubs need not be coding experts themselves. There are abundant resources available for teaching coding, setting up these clubs, structuring activities, and soliciting experienced experts. Youth and young adults have a desire to learn how to not just be a user of technology, but to become a producer of technology by understanding how it works, and how to program hardware to perform desired functions.

Mentor Programs

One of the most impactful ways to influence young adults in making choices about their future schooling and careers is through providing them with positive role models who are doing work in fields of interest. Partnering young people with mentors from STEAM fields provides them a context for what they're learning, networking opportunities, and answers to their questions from someone who has lived them. Mentors can be one-to-one partners, can be individuals volunteering to lead small group clubs or events, or can sit on panels to field questions about the how and why of teaching computer science.

Reaching Females

Much discussion about garnering interest and participation in computer sciences is centered on the gender disparity in the fields. This is an issue for adult women as well as young girls. Conjecture is that surrounding younger girls with positive role models and mentors in STEAM careers can help reverse that trend down the road.

"Every girl deserves to take part in creating the technology that will change our world, and change who runs it."—Malala Yousafszai (Code.org n.d.)

There are organizations that are working hard to provide opportunities for females of all ages to engage in programming clubs and activities, to see the relevance of programming to their lives, and to find mentors to follow.

A very popular book series is paving the way for young women to become scientists, engineers and designers at a very young age. *Rosie Revere, Engineer*; *Iggy Peck, Architect*; and *Ada Twist, Scientist*—all written by Andrea Beatty—are the fictionalized children's stories behind such prominent figures as Rosie the Riveter and Ada Lovelace, the woman credited with the first published application of programming fundamentals, long before the rise of computers in our society. There are also downloadable discussion questions and activities to accompany these books as they are used to reinforce the roles of females in the history of STEM.

Google has a page called Made with Code on which it houses projects that involve programming (everything from simple to complex) in fields like art, graphic design,

Figure 9.1. It is important to offer programming to the underrepresented populations in our communities. *Courtesy of potus-cs.jpg*

fashion, architecture, and music. There is also a section of the page that functions as a database of mentors.

Many companies are also producing games and kits specifically aimed toward females wanting to explore coding and STEM. One of the more familiar ones is called Goldie-Blox, in which materials and instructions are provided to apply engineering and design concepts to build a specified creation. There are also books to accompany the kits.

Organizations like Girls Who Code are partnering with communities and corporations to set up coding clubs for girls, particularly in urban and lower-income areas. One of the states that has embraced this most enthusiastically is the state of Texas, where girls' coding clubs are becoming more and more common, thanks in large part to an organization called Girl Start (n.d.) that is involved in setting up these clubs. In the suburban Milwaukee area in Wisconsin, technical schools like Milwaukee School of Engineering and University of Wisconsin, Waukesha, partner with an organization called GEMS (Girls in Engineering, Math, and Science) to sponsor events during the year including codeathons and classes for female teens and preteens.

On a more global level, organizations like Tech Girls sponsor summer exchange programs that allow girls from areas such as the Middle East and Africa to interact with role models and train for skills that will allow them to pursue careers in STEM fields around the world.

In the United States, the NCWIT (National Council for Women in Technology) is a national nonprofit organization specifically aimed at increasing involvement of females in technology. NCWIT (n.d.) works to maintain lists of resources and contacts; develop activities and programs; and act as a liaison between schools, libraries, and businesses to encourage and support programs for girls in technology. They also have subprograms geared at women of color, women just entering the work force, and women looking to become mentors for others.

Reaching Non-English Speakers or Nonverbal Individuals

For learners entering our programs who do not speak English as their primary language, we can provide them with a way to express their creativity and their abilities without the barrier of English fluency. The letters and symbols used in a text-based coding language will mean the same thing, regardless of who is writing the code, so using a translator to allow them to understand written directions would be the only necessity in order to give them the same opportunity for learning as all other participants.

> "Coding is today's language of creativity. All our children deserve a chance to become creators instead consumers of computer science."—Maria Klawe, President of Harvey Mudd College (Code.org n.d.)

The same can be said for nonverbal learners, whether children or young adults. The ability to take an idea and make it come to life, either on a screen or through a creation like a robot, can be liberating for those who are not able to communicate these ideas verbally. With younger children who are nonverbal, block programming languages like Scratch work very well. The touch-and-drag motion is easy enough for even learners with underdeveloped fine motor skills or limited muscle control to perform, particularly if they have a stylus available to assist them. More importantly, learning how to program allows all people to participate in an activity that engages and challenges their minds and allows them to express creatively.

Alongside the push to get more females engaged in programming and computer science, there is a similar push to get youth in urban areas or low-economic areas similarly engaged. There are many grant opportunities available to fund programs that will specifically impact youth in disadvantaged areas. There are also many options for partnering with schools and public organizations like recreation centers, before-school and after-school drop-off programs, or adult education centers. Every member of the community deserves the same career preparation and learning opportunities, so offering programming in public institutions is very important. Equally as important is to work on establishing connections for them, either with mentors, guest speakers, program teachers, or even just biographies of people in STEM and programming careers who look like them—gender, skin color, and cultural dress. This makes the goal of learning computer science seem even more attainable for them.

⑥ School Partnerships

Often, when creating a program in a public library, it is not seen as connected with the public schools. There can be many benefits, however, achieved by partnering schools and libraries together to provide computer science programming in the community. Particularly when planning programming, it is helpful for libraries to know what schools are offering, and vice versa. The calendar can be arranged, too, so that a program is offered at

Table 9.1. Activity Ideas for Partnering with Schools

	MATH	SCIENCE	SOCIAL STUDIES
Activity Ideas	• Using a number line • Measuring and classifying angles • Coordinate graphing • Drawing shapes • Sequence—making patterns	• Animate the water cycle • Animate life cycle of a butterfly • Animate cause-and-effect relationships (states of matter, chemical changes) • Code projects with circuitry, sound, and light	• Directions—points on a compass • Maps • Understanding events on a timeline • Animate migration • Animation of a famous historical figure • Animation of a prominent local person
	ART	**READING**	**WRITING**
Activity Ideas	• How to draw . . . • Architecture • Lines, angles, precision of shapes • Color • Patterns repeated • Time-lapse photography	• Comparing coding languages • Book study—history of computer science, biography of famous computer scientists, computer scientists from underrepresented populations • Characters—dress your bot as different characters • Plot—sequence and order • How to read code for errors	• If . . . then . . . statement • Cause-and-effect statements • Procedural writing • Writing with specific detail • How-to guides • Forming letters • Technical writing as a genre • Sequence

the library after introductory lessons have been covered in the schools. The annual Hour of Code is a great starting point for that. Events can be coordinated between the schools, and the libraries can emphasize to participants that this is not just a school subject.

In order to create opportunities for connection among community members, a city-wide event, like a codeathon or a cross-town problem-solving challenge, can give participants an opportunity to share with each other. Including participants in the schools might be a wonderful opportunity to connect youth with mentors who are right nearby. They might make connections that would allow them a chance to job-shadow in order to determine a career field of interest.

Library coding programs can also support the schools by extending on topics taught in the schools through integrated coding projects. There are dozens of possibilities for simple, engaging projects that reinforce concepts or facts learned in school, using the programs and equipment already in place. See table 9.1 for activity ideas related to partnering with schools.

ⓖ Community Partnerships

As mentioned earlier, funding and staffing can often be barriers for setting up programs, particularly if a library is starting from scratch, with no devices or equipment designated for the program. Reach out to the community and form partnerships. These partnerships do not have to be one-sided. A coding program, funded by a company or an organization, could be created around the idea of designing something to solve a problem within the organization or community. Corporations in the STEM fields may be interested in partnering to start a program with the intent of providing training to individuals who would later serve as interns for the company. They may also be able to donate materials and tools in exchange for receiving public credit (free advertising!) from you. Computer science education is not just limited to libraries and schools. There are many other players in the community who are interested in seeing quality programming grow.

⊚ Global Connections

Code Club International offers a network of coding clubs from around the world. As of publication, there were over ten thousand code clubs registered with the organization, representing twelve different countries. This organization connects registered clubs for global collaboration, but it also maintains a library of activities *and* translates them into multiple languages. Their mission is to get every kid in every country coding, and in order to make that happen they are providing the resources that teachers and librarians would need. The activities are geared toward nine- to thirteen-year-olds and are free to use, with the stipulation that the clubs are offered free to participants. If a library would like to host a club but doesn't have someone to lead it, Code Club International works to pair them up with a volunteer who will come to their venue to run the club.

Every year Code.org asks participants to register for the Hour of Code in order to allow participants to connect and see how many groups from all around the world are doing the same activities. Programmers, regardless of where they are, can know that children and young adults from so many countries and continents are engaging in the same activities as they are.

Each January, We Connect the Dots (n.d.), an organization based in New York, sponsors the International Code-A-Thon, in which teams from around the world analyze global issues and work together to come up with a solution. One of their missions is to reach out to a diverse population from many different parts of the world. A good number of children and young adults have limited exposure to other countries, other cultures, and other parts of the world. Activities that help them understand that children everywhere are a lot like them will improve their global and cultural awareness as well as helping them feel connected to people so far away.

Regardless of where they come from, what they look like, where they live, how old they are, or how much experience they've had in the past, everyone deserves the opportunity to learn and grow through computer science instruction. With every passing year, the availability of tools and materials to make this happen grows, so the availability of quality programming education should continue to grow as well.

The increase in technology use, in schools, libraries, and businesses, is only going to continue. It is vital that we help children and young adults keep up with the trend. By starting their computer science education early, and continuing it consistently throughout their childhood and adolescence, we will find greatly increasing numbers of proficient programmers ready to enter the workforce. These may be the very people who design and program the next great technology that will change our lives.

⊚ Key Points

- Coding is a way to reach our communities' underrepresented populations.
- Libraries and schools can partner together for coding programming.
- Businesses and corporations are often interested in working with libraries and schools to provide computer science programming.
- Coding clubs are a great opportunity for global awareness and connections.

⊚ Resources

Code Club International—http://www.Codeclubworld.org

Level Up Village—http://www.levelupvillage.com. STEM activities with global partnerships

⊚ References

Code.org. N.d. "Leaders and Trend-Setters All Agree on One Thing." Retrieved from https://code.org/quotes.

GirlStart. N.d. Home page. Retrieved from http://girlstart.org/.

National Center for Women & Information Technology. N.d. "Who We Are." Retrieved from https://www.ncwit.org/about/who.

We Connect the Dots. N.d. Home page. Retrieved from http://we-connect-the-dots.org/.

Appendix A

Starting a Coding Program

What you need in order to start a coding program:

- Coaches, teachers, or facilitators
  - Knowledgeable in whatever coding language is being used
  - Motivating and inspiring
  - Outgoing and friendly
  - Connected to the library or to a contact person or liaison to coordinate with the logistics of the offering
  - Ideally matched with participants at a ratio of one facilitator to five participants (more than one facilitator if you're looking at hosting younger kids)
- Participants
  - Determine what age and how many for the particular offering
  - Unite around a specific interest
- Curriculum
  - What will they be learning or doing?
  - On devices or unplugged?
  - Challenge based or project based?
  - Introduction to the language, or a deep dive into it?
- Venue
  - Conference room, classroom, or public space (recreation center, for example)
  - Easily accessible to participants
  - Able to accommodate the demand on wireless or Internet connection
  - Large enough for expected number of participants
  - Reasonable cost or free (If there is a cost, planners will need to determine who will pay that cost or if it will be shared by all participants.)
- Devices
  - Provided? Or bring your own?
  - Are charging stations or ports available?

- If participants are bringing their own devices, provide very specific information ahead of the offering, specifying what programs, apps, browsers, plug-ins, or operating systems will be needed. (Offer times ahead of the event to have participants bring in devices to check that they will work, if possible.)
- Is there someone available on-site to help with technical issues?

Appendix B

Planning a Coding Project

Name:

Project title:

Coding program to be used:

What will I be controlling with the coding?

Materials:

What do I need to learn in order to do this project?

Procedure:

Appendix C

Planning Template for Building a Web Page

PAGE TITLE	LEVEL	CONTENT: TEXT	CONTENT: MEDIA
	Home—Top Level		
	Level 2—Under Home		

Appendix D

Evaluating an Online Coding Course

- Is it compatible with multiple web browsers?
- Is there a cost?
- Does it start at an introductory level?
- Is it self-paced?
- Does it provide options for both hacking prewritten code and for writing code from scratch?
- Does it include explanations for the different symbols, words, or variables used?
- Does it teach why, not just how?
- Does it provide explanations for errors instead of just correcting them?
- Does it go up to an advanced level?

Appendix E
Game Making Planner

Name:

Game title:

Game-making platform to be used:

What is the objective?

Who are the characters?

How do you play?

Will there be multiple levels? How will you get to a higher level?

How do you win/lose?

Appendix F
Coding Card Arrow

Figure F.1. Arrow cards can be used to teach coding without devices when working with beginning learners.

Index

About the Author

Wendy Harrop has been a public school teacher for twenty-two years. She taught in the classroom for eleven years, in Illinois, California, and Wisconsin. Most recently, she has been a technology integrator and gifted specialist in the Oconomowoc Area School District, in Oconomowoc Wisconsin, where she has worked for eleven years. Her focus is on integrating technology in education, particularly in the area of makerspaces. She worked with a team to design and implement a makerspace in her K–4 school in 2013, and since then has become passionate about integrating making and STEAM, particularly computer programming, across the curriculum. She resides in Waukesha, Wisconsin, with her husband, also an educator, and her two sons.

CPSIA information can be obtained
at www.ICGtesting.com
Printed in the USA
BVHW01s1733220618
519690BV00003B/4/P